Contents

KOPI, COFFEE & CRAFT

A PERSONAL BREW OF SINGAPORE'S COFFEE SOUL

SUHAIMI SUKIMAN

INDIA · SINGAPORE · MALAYSIA

ISBN

Hardcase 979-8-89906-560-6
Paperback 979-8-89777-382-4

Foreword 1

As artistically outlined to the reader, Singapore coffee culture rightfully embraces history, tradition, innovation, and variety, avoiding any attempt to say that newer is better. This book perfectly navigates the reader through the delicate balance between old versus new brewing methods and the art versus science of coffee construction.

Throughout my time in the industry, it has become my firm belief that a great coffee transcends the product and becomes an experience, an opportunity to connect, collaborate, and create. This experience is only made possible by the barista and their tools, underwritten by the quality of the ingredients and the skill of the professional.

Just over 10 years ago, an ambitious Australian roastery, Toby's Estate, spread its wings from Australia to Singapore. I had the privilege to work alongside Suhaimi during that time, a time that filled us with our fair share of stress, deep learning, joy, and discovery. The success of that venture today lies in no small part to Suhaimi's unwavering work ethic.

Reflecting on that time, I am reminded of a quote: "Motivation is what gets you started, but commitment is what keeps you going." - Jim Rohn.

To the coffee industry, to his family, to his friends, to his faith, and to mastering the perfect cup, Suhaimi embodies the true meaning of commitment.

He has dedicated his entire career to inspiring everyone he has trained or worked alongside to elevate coffee beyond the cup. For that, and for sharing such a personal journey of Singapore's coffee culture, on behalf of all coffee lovers, I say thank you. We raise a cup to you.

– Andrew Low
Chief Executive Officer
Coffee Supreme

Foreword 2

I really appreciate Suhaimi and his continual push to learn and share knowledge with the global barista and specialty coffee community. Some of his articles from 2015 were among the first published on Perfect Daily Grind during its early years. They provided concise knowledge that was simply not available at the time and played a key role in driving the barista community forward.

I'm delighted to see that he is now publishing a book just under a decade later and sharing his knowledge with an ever wider audience.

– Henry Wilson
Founder
Perfect Daily Grind | PDG Media | Producer & Roaster Forum | Coffee Intelligence

INTRODUCTION

A Journey Through Singapore's Coffee Heritage

In the heart of a town in Singapore, among rows of old shophouses painted in pastel hues, was the house where I first learned to appreciate the essence of coffee. The building had stood for years, its wooden shutters slightly warped from the afternoon sun, with high ceilings and a narrow, tiled corridor lined with bicycles resting against peeling walls. The kitchen, always busy and warm, opened up to a small back alley where cats lounged lazily in the afternoon sun. It was here that my grandfather, Atuk, introduced me to the ritual of morning coffee.

Atuk was a man of few words but many routines. Each morning, as the town awoke, he would prepare his kopi-o with great care. The coffee was strong, its rich scent filling the house even before the kettle began to whistle. He poured the brew into a chipped porcelain cup, the one with faded blue flowers around the rim. But instead of drinking it straight from the cup, he would transfer the steaming liquid into a wide, melamine saucer. This, he claimed, helped the coffee cool to the perfect sipping temperature, and also allowed the aroma to unfurl more fully, a scent that recalled earth and fire.

I watched him from across the table, mesmerized by the precision of his movements. Atuk's hands, wrinkled and steady, never spilt a drop as he lifted the saucer to his lips, pausing for a moment to savour the smell. It was a sacred pause, a silent communion with his cup before the morning turned into chatter as the rest of the household joined him.

The conversations around the table ranged wide, from the mundane to the profound. The rising cost of fish, the latest political developments, stories pulled from the morning's newspaper that lay open beside Atuk. The adults' voices mixed into a comforting murmur, punctuated now and then by Atuk's quiet chuckles or affirming nods.

In the cooler hours of the afternoon, Atuk's ritual would move to the front of the house. There, by the open door, he sat cross-legged on a faded mat, his back straight as a rod, the newspaper spread before him on the floor. With the same porcelain cup refilled and resting within arm's reach, he would sip slowly between paragraphs, his eyes scanning the newsprint, completely absorbed.

Watching him over the years, first as a wide-eyed boy and then as a teenager, I slowly began to understand that coffee was more than a drink. It was the quiet moments before the world stirred. It was the way voices softened over a shared cup, and the way routines shaped the day. It was the conversations that stretched long after the last sip, the unspoken companionship in a familiar ritual. Coffee was about the experience, community, culture, and, as I would come to realize later, a craft that had evolved into something deeply intricate: specialty coffee.

As I grew older, I noticed that my father, Ayah, had his own way with coffee, one that was different from Atuk's yet carried the same sense of devotion. If Atuk's ritual was calm and careful, Ayah's was firm. He would set up his small station in the kitchen, the counters lined with glass jars filled with ground coffee, each one labeled in his neat handwriting. His thermos was an odd-looking thing, slightly dented from years of use, with a small detachable cup as its lid. I can still see him unscrewing it with ease, pouring out the thick black liquid in a steady stream before taking the first sip with an almost satisfied sigh. It didn't matter where he was, whether at home, at work, or on one of his fishing trips by the coast; his coffee was always with him.

Even though I was there, even though I watched him almost daily, coffee was never something we shared back then. It belonged to him, much like Atuk's kopi ritual had belonged to him. It wasn't until I became an adult, and later a father myself, that coffee became something we truly shared.

In my early twenties, every weekend, we would sit together, brewing and sipping a simple cup of kopi, often made at home. The routine became familiar. Ayah would set out the essentials: the coffee, the kettle, and the well-worn cups that had seen years of conversations. Sometimes, we sat by the kitchen table, the surface still slightly damp from being wiped down after breakfast. Other times, we took our cups to the veranda. It was during these moments, in the stillness between sips, that our conversations stretched. Ayah would talk about the week, about work, about a fishmonger at the market who had tried to overcharge him for tenggiri. I would listen, nodding as I swirled the last dregs of kopi in my cup.

One morning, as he set down his cup, I placed an espresso in front of him, a small, unassuming shot in a thick ceramic demitasse. He eyed it curiously, lifting it to his nose before taking a careful sip. I watched as his expression changed from a slight frown to a thoughtful pause.

"Wah, this one's got a sharp kick," he finally said, rolling the taste on his tongue.

I laughed, nodding. "Different, right? No sugar, no milk, just the beans. It is a lighter roast, so the acidity comes out more."

And just like that, the weekend coffee sessions became something more. I introduced him to flat whites, explaining how the milk was steamed to a silky texture, and how it balanced the espresso without drowning out its character. We talked about tasting notes, and how some beans carried hints of citrus, while others had a nuttier, chocolatey depth. He listened, nodding occasionally, always curious.

It was during one of these mornings, between sips of kopi and quiet understanding, that I finally shared my plan, the idea that had been weighing on me for months. I wanted to leave my stable, high-paying job. I wanted to take a risk, step into the unknown, and chase something that might fail. I wanted to be a co-owner of a young local brand and run my own coffee business!

Thinking back to these coffee moments with my father, I see how our stories are part of something bigger, something that has shaped Singapore over time. Coffee has always been more than a drink here; it is a part of the city's soul.

From the dark, robusta-heavy cups of kopi-o in traditional kopitiams to the delicate single-origin pour-overs in modern specialty cafés, every brew here carries stories of migration, adaptation, and evolution. This city, a global crossroads, has never been bound to a single coffee tradition. Instead, it has absorbed and reshaped influences over centuries. The Chinese and Hainanese migrants, arriving in the late 19th and early 20th centuries, brought with them the early kopitiams, simple, no-frills coffee houses where thick, bold kopi was roasted with butter and sugar for extra body and depth. The Indian Muslim migrants introduced their own traditions, with teh from sarabat stalls offering a different kind of communal gathering space, where conversations flowed as easily as the frothy chai. European colonialists, accustomed to a different kind of coffee culture, introduced yet another layer, favoring darker roasted beans and simple black brews. The city took these influences and made them its own.

For much of the 20th century, kopi culture thrived, firmly rooted in daily life. It was the drink of the working class, affordable and deeply familiar, served in thick ceramic cups on marble-topped tables where hawkers and businessmen, students and retirees all sat shoulder to shoulder. As Singapore moved Into the late 20th and early 21st centuries, its coffee culture took on a new shape. By the late 2000s, a different kind of café was emerging, influenced by the global specialty coffee movement. These new spaces focused on high-quality beans, lighter roasts that emphasized natural flavors, and precise brewing techniques that turned coffee into art. Baristas carefully weighed, ground, and extracted each shot with precision, treating coffee like a science.

Yet, traditional kopitiams have never faded amidst this evolution. The uncles at the kopitiam still poured kopi from long-spouted metal kettles into well-worn cups, still shouted orders in rapid-fire lingo, and remembered their customers by drink preference rather than by name. The coexistence of kopitiams and contemporary cafés is a clear example of Singapore's ability to hold on to its past while stepping forward into the future. Walking through the city, it is easy to see this balance. A specialty coffeehouse, minimalist in design, sits just a few doors down from a decades-old kopitiam. Office workers grab a flat white to go, while the older generation lingers over a kopi C, both drinks brewed with the same intention: to pause, to reflect, to savor. Singapore's coffee scene is built on these diverse layers, each one adding depth to how we understand and appreciate our daily cup.

My own journey with coffee has been just as layered. What began with an innocent sip from my grandfather's saucer turned into years of learning, working, and slowly building a career in the industry. Before I ever thought about running a coffee company, I spent years behind the counter, in roasting rooms, and on the road, immersing myself in every aspect of the craft.

Eight of those years were with Starbucks, where I started as a part-time barista, thinking it would be a temporary job. Instead, I found myself drawn deeper into the world of coffee, rising through the ranks until I left as a Coffee Ambassador in 2007. The fast-paced environment demanded precision, learning to extract espresso shots consistently, texturing milk to the right level of smoothness, and understanding how to maintain quality even during the busiest morning rushes. But beyond the technical side, Starbucks taught me something else: the power of coffee to bring people together. The small interactions at the counter, the regular customers whose orders I memorized, and the way a well-made cup could turn someone's day around.

After Starbucks, I stepped into a different side of the industry, spending four years working in a traditional coffee shop and roastery, Hui Yee Coffee, later rebranded as Cuppachoice Coffee. Here, the focus shifted from lattes and caramel macchiatos to robusta beans, metal kettles, and kopi brewing techniques that had remained unchanged for generations. The roasting room was always warm, filled with the sharp, smoky scent of coffee beans caramelizing in thick drums. I learned the difference between brewing commercial-grade arabicas and pulling kopi with the effortless speed of someone who had done it a thousand times before. I found beauty in the balance of a well-brewed kopi C kosong, its flavors simple yet deeply familiar.

Four more years followed with Sydney-based coffee company Toby's Estate, which set up a shop and a roastery in Singapore. This was where I saw the bridge between traditional and specialty coffee come to life. I worked alongside people who spoke about coffee with the same reverence as a winemaker speaks of grapes, exploring processing methods, elevation, and how a single farm's harvest could taste wildly different depending on the roast. It was here that I learned about sourcing, about direct relationships with farmers, and about how the choices made at origin shaped every cup poured in a café thousands of miles away.

Each of these experiences shaped the way I saw coffee, as a craft, a connection, and a culture that stretched far beyond a single cup. I sat down to pen these pages and take readers on a journey through that world, blending personal storytelling with industry insights and cultural exploration. Whether you are a coffee professional, an aspiring entrepreneur, or someone who simply enjoys a well-made cup, this book will offer a fresh perspective on what coffee means in Singapore. It is a story of tradition and change, of old methods meeting new ideas, of the everyday moments that make coffee more than a drink.

Each chapter explores a different part of this story. We begin with the enduring legacy of kopi, a drink that has remained a constant even as the city has transformed. We look at its history, the way it is brewed in traditional kopitiams, and why it continues to be a daily staple despite the growing presence of specialty coffee. From there, we follow the evolution of Singapore's coffee culture, shaped by global influences, the rise of third-wave coffee, and the shift toward independent cafés that focus on sourcing, craft, and experience.

Beyond the drinks themselves, this book tells the stories of the people behind the counter and beyond it: the baristas who have mastered their craft, the roasters who bring out the best in every bean, and the entrepreneurs who have taken risks to create something new. These individuals have helped shape Singapore's coffee scene, elevating standards, introducing new flavors, and reimagining what a coffee space can be.

But behind the perfectly pulled espresso shots and busy kopitiams lies a world of challenges. I learned early on that running a coffee business in Singapore is nothing like the romanticized idea of opening a café and serving coffee all day. Every thriving coffee shop faces a daily struggle, dealing with rising rents, changing consumer habits, and the constant challenge of maintaining consistency in an industry with tight margins and high expectations. Singapore moves fast. A café can open to great fanfare one month and quietly close the next. Trends shift overnight. Customers look for novelty but still expect familiarity. There is no room for complacency.

I've seen these challenges firsthand, both in my journey and in the experiences of café owners, roasters, and baristas who have poured everything into their craft. Through conversations, reflections, and the lessons I've gathered over the years, this book shares the realities of finding a way through this industry, the mistakes that became learning curves, the unexpected turns, and the quiet victories that made it all worthwhile. There are lessons in every step, from securing the right location to understanding the delicate balance of pricing and perception. The long hours, the unpredictability of customer traffic, and the constant need to adapt make it a business that demands everything. For those who love it, there is no other place they'd rather be.

But beyond the technicalities of running a café, this book is about passion. It is about the love for a drink that has remained constant, even as the world around it has changed. I think of the uncles at the kopitiam, the ones who wake before dawn, their hands moving with practiced ease as they pull kopi with the same technique they have used for decades. I think of the young baristas standing behind sleek espresso machines, adjusting grind size and water temperature, chasing the perfect balance in a single shot.

And then there is the coffee itself, the quiet alchemy that happens when hot water meets freshly ground beans, releasing a rich and familiar aroma that lingers in the air. The moment of pause before that first sip and the warmth spreading through fingers wrapped around the cup.

At the heart of it all, this book is about you, the reader. Coffee, in all its forms, has a way of bringing people together, and no matter what led you to these pages, you have a place in this story. Maybe you are here to trace the roots of kopi culture, to understand how it has endured through generations. Maybe you are curious about the specialty coffee movement and how it reshaped the café scene in Singapore. Or perhaps you are looking for something more personal, insights into what it takes to build a life around coffee, to turn passion into a craft, and a craft into a livelihood.

Whatever brings you to these pages, I invite you to step into this world with me. Grab a coffee, settle in, and let's begin.

Barista
onship
rch 2011

PURA Milk

CAFE e NATA
CAFÉ e NATA
MARGARET's
CAFE e NATA

CONFESSIONS OF A BARISTA

IMPORTANT TRAIT: Mr Suhaimie Sukiman says being able to hold a conversation with just about anyone is an important trait of a good barista. TNP PHOTO: ARIFFIN

He's a rock star coffee maker

Certified sensory judge can't enjoy cup in cafe without being recognised by fellow baristas

BENITA AW YEONG
benitaay@sph.com.sg

When it comes to coffee, you could say that Mr Suhaimie Sukiman is one of the best.

Today, the 32-year-old is a certified sensory judge at the World Barista Championships, a renowned international coffee competition.

There are only 43 such judges in the world. He is also a certified latte art judge and will be one of the judges at the Singapore National Barista Championship next month.

The popularity of latte art, where baristas create designs on a cup of coffee, has glamorised the job, but Mr Suhaimie says that dedication to mastering the fundamental principles is key.

He picked up the trade when he was 16, at a global chain which has many outlets in Singapore.

"I was skateboarding in the CBD and I saw a sign that they were hiring. I went and tried for the job and fell in love with it in my first year," he says.

To be certified as a sensory judge at the world championships, he had to pass two exams and perform well at two practical assessments.

"One of them involved blind-tasting 26 cups of coffees, some of which had multiple flavours in one. I had to identify at least 22 correctly," he says.

To raise his chances, he quit smoking and cut down on spicy food so that his palate would be as clean and sensitive as possible.

The sacrifices paid off when he was one of the eight in his cohort to be certified, out of 26 people last year.

Barista hopefuls often attend courses at Toby's Estate – an Australian cafe off Rodyk Street, where Mr Suhaimie is now the coffee operations manager – where they hope to do latte art without mastering the basics.

"When they can't even pull a shot or froth milk properly, latte art gets very frustrating because it's about getting the right colour and creating perfect symmetry," says the veteran.

To master the pulling of a coffee shot, trainees undergo three hours of theory lesson and spend about one month practising.

"If they have a keen learning attitude, we may accelerate their progression. Often, a barista not only makes the coffee, but doubles as dishwasher and waiter. That's something most people don't see," he says.

While coffee remains the source of his passion, being a barista is about being in the "people business", he says.

Some customers get so attached to their favourite barista that they turn into divas when they are served by someone they are not familiar with, he adds.

"I had a regular customer who rejected three cups of coffee made by a colleague of mine.

"I was in the back room and got wind of the commotion. I told him I would make him a cup, but what I actually did was to take the third cup, fiddle with it behind the counter, before bringing it back to the guy.

"He told me it tasted like a million bucks," he says.

Being able to hold a conversation with just about anyone is also an important trait of a good barista, he says.

"Multitasking is important. You have got to be able to make coffee and talk to people at the same time. All the better if you can tell the customer about the coffee beans' origins, down to the number of daughters its farmer has," he adds.

"You get a really great sense of satisfaction when you make someone's gloomy day better," he says.

A couple of local celebrities he f
personality Najib Ali and model-VJ D

He has had his fair share of diffic

A particularly memorable incid
customer who asked for the freshest

"I brought out all the bagels we
prod and pinch them while they we
wrap, because she was so adamant

"Still, she was not satisfied with
that they were very hard and threw
face," he recalls.

Under pressure to be a good e
were looking up to him, Mr Suhaim
and embarrassment and said: "You

But what happened next warm
customer who witnessed what h
ward to comfort me and actually
he says.

Despite the long hours, most
feet, there are perks to the job.

Coffee brought him and his w
was a barista at a cafe he worked
gramme executive. They have a

Mr Suhaimie has come a lon
about five to six times the $1,200

He is such a rock star in the
can't enjoy a cup in a cafe witho
low baristas.

"Some of them feel stressed
me a cup. They get a colleague
treasure it when I can walk in
he says.

But if you think his ambition
be wrong.

"My dream is to open a sho
It's seriously to-die-for," he says.

CHAPTER 1

The Heartbeats of Kopitiam Culture

Some memories stick with you, vivid and warm, no matter how much time has passed. This particular one takes me back to a leisurely Saturday morning from my childhood. The cozy smell of kaya toast filled the house, mingling with the rich aroma of kopi brewing in the kitchen. Atuk sat in his usual spot at the table, fully absorbed in his morning coffee routine. The rest chatted quietly, letting the morning slowly come to life around us.

I sat there, watching, my eyes fixed on the black liquid resting in his delicate bone china cup. The cup itself had a history of its own, its edges worn from years of use. In the soft morning light, It looked almost regal, with steam curling up lazily as if in no rush to disappear.

"Atuk, may I have some?" The words left my mouth before I had fully thought them through. My fingers gripped the edge of the table, anticipation building as I pointed toward his kopi-o, still piping hot.

Atuk looked up, his usual reserved expression softening just slightly. "Boleh, but just a little, okay," he said, his voice carrying the quiet authority of someone who had repeated these words many times before.

He reached for the cup, steady hands tilting it just enough to pour the dark liquid into a well-worn melamine saucer. The kopi spread thin across its surface, the steam rising in delicate swirls. Without a word, he slid it across the table toward me, his eyes watching for my reaction.

I reached for the saucer, my small fingers wrapping around its edges, the warmth pressing gently into my skin. Lifting it carefully, I brought it to my lips, trying to imitate the effortless way the adults around me sipped their coffee in between conversations about the news, the price of goods at the market, and the latest shifts in politics.

The first sip was a surprise. The bold bitterness hit my tongue immediately, unexpected and sharp. But then, as it settled, there was something else, the familiar sweetness of cane sugar weaving its way through the intensity, making it oddly soothing. I let the taste linger, my tongue trying to make sense of the flavors. It was nothing like the sweet, milky drinks I was used to. It was stronger, heavier, something that demanded to be sipped slowly.

I watched as the steam curled into the air, twisting and disappearing as the liquid cooled in the saucer. The room was filled with conversation, the clinking of spoons on porcelain, and the occasional scrape of a chair being pulled back. Yet, for a brief moment, all I could focus on was the coffee in my hands and the way it made me feel: curious, slightly overwhelmed, yet oddly proud. I didn't fully understand why the adults around me seemed to enjoy this dark, intense drink so much. But sitting there, with the warm saucer in my hands and the taste of kopi still lingering on my tongue, I made a quiet decision. If this was what being grown-up felt like, then I was drinking it too.

Soon, my weekend ritual extended beyond our kitchen. Atuk started bringing me along to the neighborhood kopitiam, a place that felt like an extension of home with familiar faces. There, the kopi uncle, with his warm, toothy smile and a towel slung over his shoulder, greeted us. He was a fixture at the kopitiam, known for his friendly banter and the effortless way he managed the hissing machines and boiling kettles. Each visit, he would lean over the counter, his eyes crinkling with genuine interest, and ask the same question, "Eh, so what you wanna be when you grow up?"

As a young boy, my answer changed every time. Some days, I was certain I would become a doctor. Other days, I was convinced that being a scientist was the way to go. There were moments I confidently declared that I would be a lecturer, standing in front of a classroom, teaching young minds. And then, on some mornings, when the steam from the kopi rose and I watched the uncle work with effortless precision, I told him, "Maybe I'll be a kopi master too."

He would always chuckle at my answers, nodding as if every dream I mentioned was entirely possible. I didn't know then how life would unfold, but looking back now, it's amusing to think that one of those childhood answers came true. But my story is just a small part of something much larger. To truly understand how coffee became such an integral part of my life, we first need to step back and explore the bigger picture, the story of coffee in Singapore, a journey that has shaped generations before me.

Roots of Kopi

The story of kopi in Singapore traces back to the early 20th century when waves of Hainanese migrants arrived on the island. Unlike the earlier waves of Chinese migrants, including the Hokkiens, Teochews, and Cantonese, who had already established themselves in trades like commerce, farming, and banking, the Hainanese were among the last to arrive. By the time they set foot in Singapore, most industries were already dominated by these earlier communities, leaving the Hainanese with few options. With limited opportunities, they found work where they could, mostly in the service industry, working as cooks and domestic helpers in British colonial households and Peranakan kitchens.

It was in these spaces that they picked up skills that would later define their legacy. They learned the nuances of Western dining, the techniques of British-style cooking, and, most importantly, how to brew and serve coffee the way the colonials liked it. They watched, adapted, and took what they had learned into their own kitchens, refining and modifying recipes along the way.

Then, the war came, and the years that followed were filled with uncertainty. As Singapore emerged from World War II, the economy shifted. The demand for domestic help declined, and many Hainanese workers who had once served in wealthy homes found themselves needing to carve out new paths. With experience in the kitchen but little capital to start large businesses, many turned to a concept that required few resources yet held great potential: the humble coffee shop.

And so, kopitiams were born. These simple coffee shops quickly became gathering spaces for the working class. Little did they know, these humble kopitiams would go on to become an inseparable part of Singapore's daily life.

As kopitiams took root across Singapore, another key factor shaped the way kopi was made and consumed: the city's role as a central trading port. Positioned along the Strait of Malacca, Singapore was a natural hub for goods moving between the East and the West. Spices, textiles, and tea passed through its shores, and among these commodities, coffee flowed steadily into the city. Beans arrived from neighboring regions like Indonesia and Malaysia, ensuring that Singapore had a steady supply to fuel its growing coffee culture.

Long before coffee reached Singapore, it had already established deep roots in the region. As early as the 17th century, Dutch colonial rulers introduced Arabica coffee plants to Java, turning the Indonesian islands into one of the first large-scale coffee-producing regions outside of Arabia and Ethiopia. Malaysia, though a smaller producer, played its part in this regional coffee trade. While its coffee farms never reached the scale of Indonesia's, its proximity to Singapore made it an essential supplier.

Ships carrying sacks of coffee beans from Indonesia and Malaysia would arrive at the busy docks, where laborers worked seamlessly, unloading cargo under the sun. Some of the beans were re-exported, making their way to Europe and other parts of Asia, but a significant portion stayed in Singapore, feeding the local market. The city's growing appetite for coffee meant that roasters and kopitiams had a reliable supply, allowing them to perfect their craft and develop a style of coffee that became distinctively Singaporean.

With kopi established as an everyday staple, it's impossible to talk about its significance without stepping into the roasting rooms where its bold flavors were born. My first experience inside a traditional kopi roastery was nothing like what I had expected. I had imagined gleaming machines and precise temperature controls, but what I found instead was a space that felt both raw and rhythmic, where coffee was a craft shaped by instinct, muscle memory, and the weight of tradition.

Large woks sat over open flames, their surfaces slick with melted margarine as kopi roasters worked swiftly, stirring the beans in steady, practiced motions. There was no measuring, no digital timers, just sight, sound, and smell guiding the process. The beans crackled as they turned darker, coated in a glossy layer of caramelization. I watched as the roasters tilted the heavy woks, pouring the glistening beans onto cooling trays, steam rising in soft plumes as they spread them out evenly.

Unlike the Arabica beans that Western cafés prided themselves on, lightly roasted to highlight delicate floral or fruity notes, kopitiam coffee relied on something different. The beans used were robusta or liberica, known for their intensity, bitterness, and full-bodied strength. They were chosen for their ability to deliver a strong, bold cup that could cut through the richness of condensed milk or stand on its own, unyielding and unapologetic.

The roasting process itself had its own layered history. Some believed it was a necessity born from post-war shortages, a way to make lower-quality beans taste richer when fresh, high-grade coffee was hard to come by. Others, including the kopi roasters I worked with, shared a more practical explanation rooted in economics. Roasting coffee naturally caused weight loss, with a kilogram of raw green beans shrinking by nearly 20% after roasting. For business owners looking to make the most of their inventory, this loss mattered. To counter it, roasters began adding sugar, margarine, and sometimes even grains like barley or maize, a method that retained more weight and created the signature caramelized depth that kopi drinkers came to love.

As kopi roasters perfected their techniques, dried barley and maize became popular additions. But handling these grains came with its own set of challenges, something I came to understand during my time in the traditional kopi roastery. The storage warehouses were lined with towering stacks of hessian and jute sacks, each packed tightly with grains or coffee beans, their rough, fibrous surfaces covered in dust from the long journeys. Moving these sacks was no easy task. Weighing up to 50 kilograms each, they had to be lifted, swung, and stacked with precision. Workers used metal hooks to grip the sacks, pulling them off trucks and onto wooden pallets with practiced ease. But no matter how careful they were, the fabric wore down over time. Even the tiniest hole was enough to let grains trickle onto the floor. It didn't take much for the problem to grow, as any spillage was an open invitation for pests.

Preventing infestations meant working with precision. Every shipment had to be inspected, damaged sacks patched up immediately, and the warehouse kept spotless. This attention to detail in kopi production extended to the ingredients themselves.

One particular instance from my time in the kopi industry stands out in this context. Commodity prices for barley and maize, the grains commonly used in kopi blends, suddenly spiked, rising higher than the cost of robusta beans. It was an unusual shift, one that caught many in the industry off guard. My boss, always pragmatic, saw an opportunity to cut costs and made a straightforward decision to remove the grain fillers entirely and switch to using 100% robusta beans.

For three months, we roasted without maize and barley, assuming that customers wouldn't notice. After all, we were still using high-quality robusta, the same beans that formed the backbone of kopi. The roasting process remained unchanged, the margarine and sugar still added for caramelization. On paper, it seemed like a small tweak, one that made financial sense.

But our customers noticed. Almost immediately, complaints started trickling in. Long-time patrons, those who had been drinking our kopi for years, insisted that something was off. Some said their usual cup tasted sharper, others found it too bitter. A few couldn't quite pinpoint what was wrong, but they knew it wasn't the same.

That was when I fully grasped how much the blended formula had shaped the identity of traditional kopi. It had never been just coffee. The standard mix had been carefully refined over decades: 50% robusta beans for strength, 25% maize and barley to soften the sharpness and add body, and the remaining 25% made up of margarine, sugar, and salt to create that familiar caramelized depth.

Without the grains, the balance was lost. The kopi became too intense and one-dimensional. Eventually, we reversed the change, returning to the original mix. Almost immediately, the complaints stopped. Customers took their first sip, nodded in approval, and carried on with their usual morning routines as if nothing had ever changed.

That experience reaffirmed something important: kopi was more than the sum of its parts. It wasn't just about the beans, but the process, the history, and the quiet agreement between those who made it and those who drank it. Every cup carried the weight of tradition, shaped over time by necessity and refined by generations of kopi roasters and drinkers who knew, instinctively, when something wasn't right.

The Wok Hei of Coffee

From this deep appreciation for the craft, another part of kopi culture that fascinated me was the idea of "wok hei," or the breath of the wok, which is key to creating the authentic flavor of traditional kopi. Much like how stir-fried noodles develop their signature taste from high heat and constant movement, kopi gets its distinct character from the careful roasting of beans in giant cast-iron woks over an open flame. This is a delicate process that requires precision. If the heat is too low, the beans stay raw and grassy. If it's too high, they burn, turning harsh and bitter.

Roasters work tirelessly, standing over roaring flames, stirring the beans with wide metal paddles in steady, practiced motions. Their movements are almost hypnotic, precise and never rushed. The flames licking the sides of the wok add depth to the beans, infusing them with an unmistakable smoky richness.

Over time, technology has changed the way kopi is roasted. Many kopi roasters now use specialized coffee roasting machines, allowing for better temperature control and consistency. Instead of roasting everything together, the coffee beans, barley, and maize are now prepared separately, ensuring each ingredient develops the right texture and flavor before being blended.

Yet, despite these advancements, the essence of the old methods remains. To honor tradition, kopi roasters still use a separate commercial wok with an automated paddle to heat the margarine, sugar, and salt mixture, an essential step in caramelizing the beans.

As the roasting process nears its final stage, timing becomes everything. The moment the beans reach their ideal color and development, they are swiftly transferred into the wok containing the hot caramel mixture. The beans sizzle as they meet the caramel, a sharp, fleeting crackle before they settle into the intense heat.

This step is critical. The beans must be stirred vigorously with wide metal paddles, ensuring that each one is evenly coated with the glossy caramel glaze. The coating adds sweetness and seals in the smoky complexity from the open-flame roasting, giving kopi its unmistakable bittersweet depth. The more even the glaze, the smoother the final brew. This is what separates a well-crafted kopi from one that falls flat.

Once coated, the beans are quickly emptied onto a cooling tray, where they are spread out in a thin layer. This halts the cooking process instantly, preventing the sugars from over-caramelizing and turning bitter. The heat escapes in waves, steam rising as the beans crackle softly, releasing their final bursts of aroma. This moment always struck me: the transition from fire and motion to stillness, the last stage before the beans rest, ready to be ground, brewed, and served.

This improved method of kopi roasting has brought greater efficiency to the process. Separating the steps has significantly reduced fire hazards, which used to be a serious concern when roasting and caramelizing were done together in a single drum. It has also allowed for a clearer division of tasks, with the roaster, caramel mixture cook, and final blender each taking on a specific role in the process.

The Kopi Choreography

The brewing process is where the final transformation of kopi happens, turning those caramelized beans into a bold, aromatic drink. Brewing kopi is an art in itself, perfected over decades by skillful hands and guided by instinct. Unlike espresso machines or pour-over drippers, kopi relies on a simple yet ingenious tool: the coffee sock. This long, reusable cloth filter is central to the brewing process, its worn fabric stained dark from years of use.

Before the brewing even begins, the sock must be carefully prepped. It is rinsed with hot water to cleanse it of any residue flavors from previous brews and to ensure it is warm and damp, ready to embrace the freshly-ground coffee. What makes the coffee sock so unique is the way its fabric affects the final cup. The tightness of its weave determines how much body and bitterness are extracted from the grounds. A looser weave allows more oils to pass through, creating a fuller, heavier mouthfeel, while a tighter weave produces a cleaner, crisper brew.

With the coffee sock warmed and ready, the next step begins. The kopi master starts by scooping freshly ground robusta beans into the sock, measuring by sight and feel rather than relying on scales or timers. The grind is medium-fine, a careful balance: fine enough to draw out the coffee's rich flavors, but coarse enough to prevent clogging the fabric. The sock, stretched over a metal ring attached to a handle, is suspended above a jug or pot, waiting for the boiling water to bring the grounds to life.

With a steady hand, the kopi master begins pouring, releasing a thin stream of water in a slow, deliberate spiral over the coffee grounds. The water, heated just shy of boiling, seeps into the coffee, saturating every particle. This first pour, known as the bloom, allows trapped gases to escape, releasing a wave of earthy, slightly smoky aromas. The grounds rise and expand for a moment before settling, signaling that they are ready for full extraction.

Patience is key here. The kopi master watches intently as the dark liquid begins to drip through the sock, filtering steadily into the vessel below. The result is smooth yet strong, carrying deep bitterness and caramelized undertones.To intensify the flavor, the process is often repeated. The freshly brewed coffee is poured back through the sock, deepening its strength with each pass. The jug is lifted high, the liquid cascading back into the sock in a controlled arc, aerating the coffee as it flows.

This balance is crucial. Let the coffee steep too long, and over-extraction makes the brew harsh and overly bitter, dulling the subtle caramelized notes. Steep it too briefly, and under-extraction leaves the kopi weak and flat, lacking the body and depth that regular drinkers expect. There is no in-between. Kopi must be bold, smooth, and strong enough to cut through the richness of condensed or evaporated milk, yet never overpowering. The discerning local palate has been shaped by generations of perfected brews, and there is little room for mistakes.

Once the concentrated brew is just right, the final step begins: the customization. This is where kopi transforms to suit individual preferences, each order reflecting a different way to enjoy the drink. Kopi, the classic version, is mixed with condensed milk, creating a thick, creamy texture and a deep sweetness that rounds out the bitterness of the coffee. For those who prefer something less sweet but still smooth, kopi-C is made with evaporated milk instead, giving it a lighter body with a more balanced flavor. And then there is kopi-O kosong, black coffee without sugar or milk, where the full strength of the brew shines through, unmasked and uncompromising. Each variation, though different, remains rooted in the same tradition.

Kopi Lingo

Just as kopi brewing is a craft honed over time, so too is the language used to order it, a unique shorthand that speaks to the cultural layers found in Singapore's coffee tradition. Standing in a kopitiam and listening to orders being rattled off, kopi-C siew dai, kopi-O kosong, kopi peng, you begin to realize that ordering coffee here is a language of its own.

The lingo of kopi is a mix of Malay, Hokkien, Cantonese, and Hainanese influences, a reflection of Singapore's multicultural identity. It evolved as a way to efficiently communicate coffee preferences in busy kopitiams, where speed was essential and regulars expected their drinks to be made exactly how they liked them.

At the heart of it is the word kopi, borrowed from Malay, which simply means "coffee." From this base, different modifiers are added to customize the drink. Kopi-O refers to black coffee with sugar, with the "O" coming from the Hokkien word orh, meaning black. If no sugar is wanted, one simply adds kosong, Malay for "empty," to the order, making it kopi-O kosong, or sugarless black coffee.

Then there is kopi-C, where evaporated milk is introduced, giving the coffee a creamy texture without the thick sweetness of condensed milk. The origin of the "C" is a topic of debate. Some say it comes from the pronunciation of "Carnation," one of the most commonly used brands of evaporated milk in kopitiams. Others believe it stems from the Hainanese word xian (鲜), meaning fresh, since evaporated milk was considered a fresher alternative to condensed milk at the time.

One of the more nostalgic and unique terms is kopi gu you, or butter coffee. This old-school variation involves adding a slab of butter to hot kopi, creating a rich, velvety texture with an unmistakable depth of flavor. The name itself comes from Hokkien, as gu you literally translates to "cow oil," referring to butter. This practice dates back to pre-war Hainanese kopitiams, where it was believed that adding butter balanced out coffee's "heaty" nature by introducing the cooling properties of fat. More practically, the butter gave kopi a luxurious mouthfeel and an added layer of caramel-like richness. While less common today, it remains a nostalgic order for those who grew up with it.

Beyond these basics, the lingo gets even more nuanced. Customers can fine-tune the sweetness of their brew using siew dai (less sugar) or gah dai (extra sugar), terms borrowed from

Cantonese. Strength adjustments come from Hokkien, with gau indicating a stronger brew and po for a weaker one. And if you prefer your coffee iced, you simply add peng, a Hokkien word meaning cold or iced. A straightforward order of kopi-C peng will get you an iced coffee with evaporated milk, while kopi-O siew dai peng means an iced black coffee with less sugar.

With just a few words, you can customize every aspect of your drink to fit your exact preference. It's a system that has been fine-tuned over time, shaped by necessity and cultural exchange. A single order, kopi-O siew dai peng, captures three different modifications in just four words. It's a code that feels natural to locals but can seem like a secret language to newcomers. Together, this lingo creates a dynamic and living language of coffee that enhances daily life in Singapore.

The Kopitiam as Singapore's Living Room

With every order placed in the familiar shorthand of kopi lingo, there is one setting that ties it all together: the kopitiam. These traditional coffee shops are where the language of kopi comes alive, where words exchanged at the counter translate into steaming cups of coffee carried to worn marble-topped tables. Kopitiams have long been the heart of Singapore's social life, offering an open and familiar space where people from all walks of life gather.

Kopitiams were never meant to be grand establishments. Their charm lay in their simplicity, a no-frills setup designed for efficiency, affordability, and comfort. For generations, they have been Singapore's living rooms, where conversations flow as freely as the coffee. At a time when the city was rapidly urbanizing, these humble coffee shops provided something invaluable: accessibility.

At their core, kopitiams welcomed everyone: rickshaw pullers wiping sweat from their brows, clerks flipping through newspapers before heading to work, businessmen in neatly pressed shirts nursing their morning kopi, and retirees meeting old friends for their daily routine of coffee and conversation. Under the slow, deliberate spin of ceiling fans, strangers sat shoulder to shoulder, their differences dissolving in the shared rituals of breakfast and caffeine.

The setup was always straightforward: Tables, often zinc-topped, were chosen for their durability and practicality. In Singapore's tropical heat, they remained cool to the touch, offering a small comfort to customers escaping the midday sun. Their surfaces, worn smooth by countless cups of kopi and the occasional careless spill, reflected years of use. The pastel-colored plastic stools that surrounded them were lightweight and easily rearranged, allowing groups to gather and shift as conversations grew or faded.

The walls told their own stories: Faded posters of Tiger Beer, teh tarik, and nostalgic advertisements for condensed milk brands like Carnation clung to the peeling paint, reminders of a time when commercial branding was straightforward and unpolished. Old calendars hung from nails, sometimes left unchanged for months. These small details were simply part of the kopitiam's everyday existence, blending into the space as naturally as the aroma of kopi brewing behind the counter.

The menu offered comforting, familiar staples: kaya toast with soft-boiled eggs, the runny yolk mixed with dark soy sauce and a dash of white pepper; nasi lemak wrapped in banana leaves, its fragrant coconut rice paired with sambal and crispy anchovies; and, of course, steaming cups of kopi, brewed with robusta beans roasted in sugar and butter. The food was simple, affordable, and deeply satisfying, a reflection of the resourcefulness of the Hainanese immigrants who had perfected these offerings over time.

For all its simplicity, the kopitiam soon became a silent witness to life's big and small moments. Business deals were sealed with a handshake over a cup of kopi-O. Heated political debates unfolded at tables sticky with condensed milk. Old friends met in the same spot for decades, their conversations picking up as if no time had passed. Even in sorrow, the kopitiam provided quiet comfort, with two people sitting side by side, sharing a pot of kopi, speaking little but understanding everything.

Years later, I found myself back in a kopitiam, but this time I wasn't just a customer. I was behind the counter, standing where the kopi uncles had stood for decades, my hands learning the motions of brewing and serving, my ears tuned to the familiar sounds of the morning rush.

The smell of roasted robusta beans, deep and slightly caramelized, wrapped itself around me like a second skin. And the regulars, those who had been coming here long before I stepped behind the counter, didn't need to place their orders. They exchanged quick nods with the kopi master, an unspoken understanding that came from years of routine.

For four years, I worked in a traditional coffee roastery, roasting beans, grinding them to the right consistency, and occasionally brewing in these kopitiams, where the pace never slowed.

I learned the craft and about the people behind it. These were people who had seen the city change around them but remained rooted in their craft, ensuring that the traditions they carried would not be lost.

But that part of my journey is another story, one that deserves its own place. Soon, we'll get there.

CHAPTER 2

Behind the Beans

Charles Dickens once wrote in *Great Expectations*, "That was a memorable day to me, for it made great changes in me. But it is the same with any life. Imagine one selected day struck out of it, and think how different its course would have been." Looking back, there is one such day in my life that I would never hope to strike out because, without it, I wouldn't have found the path that led me to where I am today.

It was 1999, a year that feels both like yesterday and a lifetime ago. Fresh in college, I was still unsure of what my future would hold. Like most students, I wasn't thinking too far ahead. I was simply trying to get through my classes, make new friends, and, in the immediate term, find a part-time job. One afternoon, a classmate named Jamal, whom I had just befriended, suggested that we look for work together. It wasn't about passion or career ambitions. We just needed extra income, and finding a job with a schedule that fit around our studies seemed like the practical thing to do.

We both lived in the west side of Singapore but attended school in the east, a daily journey that felt like an eternity. The 1.5-hour commute each way meant waking up early to catch the first bus, switching to the train, and then walking the final stretch to campus. By the time we got to class, we had already spent what felt like half a day on the road. With the long hours of travel already cutting into our time, we knew that choosing a job nearby wasn't an option. We needed to make the commute work in our favor.

So, we settled on the Central Business District (CBD). It seemed like the perfect middle ground. After school, we could head straight to work, complete a four-to-six-hour shift, and then make our way home with a much shorter commute. At that moment, the job itself didn't matter. What we wanted was convenience, something that fit into our schedules without adding too much stress.

With our freshly printed resumes in hand, passport photos carefully glued in the top corner, my friend and I stepped into the city, school uniforms slightly wrinkled from the long commute. We had no real strategy, just a quiet determination to land a job that day. The Central Business District was alive with the lunch crowd, professionals moving briskly with takeaway cups in hand. We walked with purpose, scanning storefronts, unsure of where we'd end up but ready to try anywhere that looked promising.

One of our first stops was Starbucks. Back in 1999, it still felt like a new, unfamiliar presence in Singapore. Unlike the kopitiams we had grown up with, this was a different kind of coffee culture: sleek, modern, and distinctly Western. We pushed open the glass doors, and the cool blast of air-conditioning hit us, carrying the scent of freshly brewed coffee and warm pastries.

The interior felt like a different world. The walls were lined with shelves displaying gleaming coffee beans in glossy bags, their labels showing off exotic origins like Sumatra, Guatemala, and Kenya. A long wooden counter stretched across the space, and a glass pastry case showcased muffins, croissants, and oversized cookies that looked nothing like the ones we usually saw at local bakeries.

The baristas moved effortlessly behind the counter, calling out drink orders with confidence. There was an ease about them, as if they knew exactly what they were doing, as if they had been part of this world for a long time. For a brief moment, I wondered if we had made the wrong choice, if we were aiming too high. But before that uncertainty could fully settle, we were approached by a friendly store manager with a name tag that read Aszy.

“Looking for a job?” she asked casually. We nodded, unsure of what to expect. Without hesitation, she handed each of us an application form and told us to fill them out whenever we were ready. We took our seats at a small corner table, pens in hand, the excitement slowly bubbling up.

Aszy’s voice broke through the soft noises of the café. “While you’re working on that, can I offer you and your friend a beverage?” she asked, her easy smile making the whole situation feel a little less formal.

I glanced up at the green menu board hanging a few meters away, scanning through the unfamiliar names. Everything sounded fancy: Caramel Macchiato, Caffè Mocha, Frappuccino, but what stood out to me more than the drinks were the prices. Almost every item cost more than what I had in my wallet.

A quiet panic crept in. Was this one of those polite offers where you were actually expected to pay? I wasn't sure, and I didn't want to take the risk.

Before I could decide, Jamal confidently spoke up. "I'll have a Mocha Frappuccino." He said it with such ease, like he had done this before. Later, he would tell me it was his older sister's favorite drink. At that moment, though, I was just impressed by how sure he sounded.

I, on the other hand, hesitated. My eyes darted back to the board, looking for the most affordable option. "Thank you. I'll just have an espresso. A solo espresso," I said finally, choosing the cheapest drink at $2.80. I had no idea what I was ordering, but at least I knew I could afford it if I had to.

The drinks arrived a few minutes later. Jamal's Mocha Frappuccino looked elaborate, topped with whipped cream, chocolate drizzle, and crushed ice swirling beneath the plastic dome lid. My espresso, on the other hand, was the exact opposite. A tiny, white porcelain cup sat on the saucer in front of me, filled with a dark liquid that barely covered the bottom. It looked intense, but I didn't think too much about it.

I had grown up drinking kopi-O, a drink I always associated with grown-ups, bold and strong with a lingering sweetness from the sugar. I assumed an espresso would be something like that, just another variation of coffee, familiar and comforting.

I lifted the cup, took my first sip, and immediately realized I was wrong. The taste hit me fast: sharp, bitter, almost overwhelming. There was no sugar, no soft edge to balance the intensity. It was nothing like the kopi I knew. My instinct was to grimace, but instead, I found myself weirdly liking it.

I swallowed, setting the cup back down, the bitterness lingering on my tongue. Kopi had always been a familiar presence in my life, but working with coffee? That was entirely new.

A few weeks later, I was officially hired as a part-time barista with Starbucks Singapore, stepping into a world I had never imagined myself in. My first real introduction to that world came when I arrived at Starbucks Training School at Liat Towers for my onboarding session.

Liat Towers stood tall along Orchard Road, an unmistakable part of Singapore's urban scene. It was where coffee culture was slowly taking root, where young professionals and students gathered with notebooks and paper cups, where the concept of specialty coffee was still something fresh and intriguing. Stepping inside the training school, I was immediately hit by the scent of freshly brewed coffee, rich, warm, slightly sweet from the natural oils released during brewing. The buzz of espresso machines at work mixed with the quiet chatter of conversation, creating an atmosphere that felt both busy and welcoming. The walls were lined with framed coffee maps and burlap sacks from coffee-growing regions around the world, Ethiopia, Colombia, Sumatra, each name carrying a sense of distant lands and untold stories.

Instructors stood at the front of the room, speaking with a passion that caught me off guard. I listened, taking in everything. I had walked into this job thinking I would be learning how to pull espresso shots and steam milk. I had not expected to be introduced to an entire world hidden within a single cup, a world I would come to embrace.

The journey I started at Starbucks Coffee Singapore, SQ Building, as a fresh-faced part-time barista quickly turned into something much bigger than I had anticipated. What began as a simple job after school soon became an education, one that stretched far beyond coffee-making and into leadership, training, and the culture of coffee itself.

Over the next few years, I found myself growing within the company, taking on new roles and responsibilities. I became a certified classroom facilitator, guiding new baristas through the same training I had once nervously sat through. I completed the Retail Training Store Manager program, learning the ins and outs of running a store, managing teams, and ensuring every cup met the highest standard. Then, in 2007, I earned the title of Coffee Ambassador, a recognition that solidified my place in the industry.

But as much as I had grown within the corporate coffee world, there was another part of me that was drawn to something deeper, something rooted in tradition. My next adventure took me away from the polished, structured environment of Starbucks and into the heart of a traditional family business that had been roasting and supplying kopi beans to local kopitiams since 1984. This career shift also entailed a complete change of scenery, a transition from the fast-paced nature of an international brand to the hands-on, deeply personal world of old-school coffee roasting.

With eight years of Starbucks experience behind me, I stepped into this new world as someone responsible for coffee sales and brand development. The company wanted to expand beyond their traditional kopi roasting roots, and I found myself in a position where I could help craft and grow a gourmet coffee brand from the ground up. At a time when specialty coffee was just beginning to gain traction in Singapore, I developed a coffee training program and played a role in establishing one of the country's first coffee academies, which was one of only two or three that existed at the time.

This chapter of my journey, one that I will explore in greater detail later, led to something even bigger. I became part of the company's transformation, overseeing its rebranding from Hui Yee Coffee Manufacturing Pte Ltd to Cuppachoice International Pte Ltd. In the four years I spent there, my responsibilities grew, taking me from Sales & Training Executive to Operations Director, a role that allowed me to shape the future of the business.

Perhaps the most defining part of this journey was the opportunity to co-own a small retail and academy space in the heart of Chinatown while working alongside the company's founding father. It was an experience that solidified my place in the world of coffee, bridging both the corporate and traditional worlds and giving me a perspective few others had.

But rewinding back to where it all began, that first step into Liat Towers as a young boy, eager and wide-eyed, I realize now how much more there was to learn. At the time, I thought coffee was simple. You roasted the beans, ground them, brewed them, and served a cup. But standing in that training room, listening to instructors talk about coffee with a depth I had never imagined, I realized it was anything but simple.

It started with the most profound lesson: the journey of a coffee bean. It was something I had never thought about before, but the more I learned, the more I saw the parallels between coffee and life itself. A single coffee bean, so small and unassuming, went through an incredible transformation before it ever reached a cup. It grew through seasons, endured unpredictable climates, was harvested, sorted, processed, and roasted, with each step influencing its final character.

I had never realized how much effort went into every cup before it even reached the hands of a barista. There was an entire world behind that one espresso shot, a world of farmers, pickers, traders, roasters, and brewers all playing a role in shaping its journey. Every step mattered, from the altitude where the coffee was grown to the way it was dried and roasted. I was fascinated by the alchemy of it all, how a brown bean could be transformed into a drink that sparked conversations, fueled early mornings, and even shaped entire cultures.

The Journey of a Coffee Bean

As I delved deeper into the world of coffee, I began to see how Singapore's relationship with coffee was unlike that of coffee-producing nations. Unlike Ethiopia, Colombia, or Brazil, where coffee farms stretched over vast lands, Singapore's role in coffee wasn't about cultivation; it was about trade, craft, and culture.

Our tropical climate and compact geography meant that coffee could never be grown here on a large scale. Instead, Singapore's coffee story begins long before the beans ever arrive on our shores. It starts in the highlands of Indonesia, Brazil, Vietnam, and Ethiopia, where farmers tend to coffee trees that will eventually make their way into the cups of kopi drinkers in local kopitiams and specialty coffee lovers in modern cafés.

Indonesia and Vietnam have always been key players in Singapore's coffee supply due to their close proximity and thriving coffee industries. Indonesia, with its volcanic soil and rich coffee-growing heritage, produces bold, earthy beans that have been a staple in Singapore's traditional kopi blends for generations. Vietnam, the world's largest producer of robusta beans, supplies the high-caffeine, full-bodied coffee that fuels many of our morning brews. Brazil, as the largest coffee producer in the world, brings a steady flow of high-quality Arabica, while Ethiopia, the birthplace of coffee itself, adds complexity and depth with its floral and fruity beans.

This diverse mix of imports caters to Singapore's broad spectrum of coffee preferences. Central to this global coffee network are the green bean importers, individuals who dedicate their lives to sourcing, selecting, and supplying the finest coffee beans from around the world. They act as the bridge between the coffee farms and our cups, ensuring that every batch of beans meets the expectations of both roasters and consumers. Without them, Singapore's coffee industry would not function the way it does today.

One of the importers I've had the privilege of working closely with is Mercanta Coffee, a UK-based specialty green coffee supplier. Their approach is deeply impactful: quality, transparency, and sustainability guide every decision they make. Unlike large-scale commodity coffee traders who deal in bulk shipments with little connection to the farmers behind the beans, Mercanta's approach is built on relationships. They don't just buy and sell coffee. Instead, they work directly with coffee producers, building long-term partnerships with farmers and cooperatives to ensure that the beans they source are of the highest quality and that the people behind them are fairly compensated.

This kind of sourcing is critical in an industry where coffee has long been treated as a commodity rather than a craft. In traditional coffee trading, beans are often bought and sold without much regard for where they came from, how they were grown, or whether the farmers earned a fair price. But Mercanta operates differently. They believe in traceability, in knowing exactly which farm or cooperative each lot of beans came from, and in paying prices that reflect the true value of the labor involved.

Their reach is global, working closely with producers in Latin America, Africa, and Asia to ensure that every batch of coffee aligns with both flavor preferences and ethical sourcing standards. This dedication to responsible sourcing is a necessary shift in an industry that has long struggled with issues of economic fairness and environmental sustainability. The way coffee is sourced impacts every step of the chain, from the farmer who plants the first seed to the final sip in a café. And companies like Mercanta are proving that sourcing can be done with care, integrity, and a deep respect for the people who make coffee possible.

Sourcing is the first step, but what follows is a careful selection process that requires a deep understanding of coffee's origins and the many factors that shape its flavor. Every stage of the bean's journey, from the altitude where it is grown to the way it is processed after harvesting, influences what ends up in the cup. Altitude plays a significant role. Coffee grown at higher altitude tends to have brighter acidity and more complex flavors because the cooler temperatures slow down the maturation of the beans. This slower growth allows the coffee cherries to develop more sugars, which leads to a fruitier and more vibrant cup. Beans grown at lower altitudes often have a fuller and richer body, with deeper chocolate or nutty notes. These differences do not make one better than the other, but they shape the character of the final brew.

Soil composition and climate also leave a distinct imprint on coffee. The volcanic soil of Ethiopia, the mineral-rich lands of Colombia, and the dense forests of Sumatra all influence the beans in unique ways. Even slight changes in rainfall or temperature can affect the crop, making each harvest slightly different from the last. Farmers must carefully manage these conditions to maintain consistency while also embracing the natural variations that make coffee so dynamic.

Processing methods further shape the coffee's personality. After the cherries are harvested, they go through different post-harvest techniques that affect their final taste. Washed coffees, also known as wet-processed, are fermented and rinsed to remove the outer fruit, creating a cleaner and brighter profile with more pronounced acidity. Naturally processed coffees are dried with the fruit still intact, allowing the beans to absorb more sugars from the cherry, which results in a richer and fruitier flavor with a heavier body. Honey processing, which falls between washed and natural, retains some of the sticky mucilage on the beans, producing a balanced, sweet, and slightly syrupy cup. All these elements work together to create endless variations in coffee.

Once the right beans are selected, the next step is cupping. This is when coffee professionals, myself included, assess the quality of the beans through a structured tasting process. Cupping is the industry-standard method for evaluating a coffee's acidity, body, sweetness, and aftertaste. Think of it like a wine tasting for coffee, where we get to uncover the unique balance and flavors that make each cup special.

The process starts with examining the dry coffee grounds and noting their fragrance. This step matters because aroma plays a big role in how we perceive flavor. That first whiff of the coffee can hint at what's to come, whether it has floral, fruity, nutty, or chocolatey notes. Once you pour hot water over the grounds, the coffee releases a richer aroma and provides even more clues about its flavor profile.

After brewing, we taste the coffee using a unique technique. Instead of sipping as usual, we slurp the coffee from a spoon to evenly spread it across the palate. This method helps us catch subtle differences in flavor and texture that might go unnoticed with a regular sip. We carefully evaluate everything: how the acidity balances with the sweetness, the weight of the body on the tongue, and how long the flavors linger after swallowing.

These cupping sessions help us determine the best use for each coffee. Some beans shine as single-origin offerings, showcasing their distinct characteristics, while others work better in blends that balance different flavors and strengths.

These steps reveal that creating a great cup of coffee is about achieving harmony and balance at every level. Each coffee has its own unique characteristics, shaped by its origin, altitude, and processing method. A bright, citrusy Ethiopian coffee, with its lively acidity and floral undertones, might stand beautifully on its own. However, if the goal is to craft a more rounded espresso blend, it might need the deep, chocolatey notes of a Brazilian coffee or the smooth, nutty profile of a Guatemalan bean to create a fuller and more balanced flavor.

This is where experience, expertise, and creativity come into play. Blending coffee is an art form, requiring an understanding of how different beans interact with one another. A well-crafted blend brings out the best in each component, ensuring that no single note overpowers the others. It is about finding the right proportions so that the sweetness, acidity, and body complement each other, resulting in a cup that feels complete.

Perfecting the Bean: The Art and Science of Roasting

Once the blend is finalized, the beans go through their final transformation: roasting. This is the stage where raw green coffee beans are turned into the rich, aromatic coffee we enjoy in cups around the world. Roasting requires a careful balance of heat, time, and technique, with each factor playing a vital role in unlocking the flavors hidden within the beans. It's a precise process, where even small changes in temperature or timing can significantly impact the result, shaping everything from the coffee's acidity and body to its aroma and aftertaste.

In Singapore, traditional kopi roasting has its own distinct approach, shaped by history and necessity. Robusta beans, known for their bold and bitter taste, are typically used. Instead of simply roasting the beans, they are caramelized with sugar, margarine, and sometimes grains like barley or maize. This method was originally created to increase yield and enhance flavor. Over the years, it has become a hallmark of local kopi, giving it a buttery texture, rich body, and smoky sweetness that many Singaporeans associate with their morning coffee.

In specialty coffee roasting, the approach is different. The focus is on preserving the natural characteristics of the bean rather than altering them. Roasters work to highlight the inherent flavors developed at the farm, bringing out delicate notes of fruit, florals, or chocolate depending on the bean's origin. The process requires an understanding of how each variety reacts to heat. A light roast may enhance acidity and clarity, while a darker roast deepens the body and intensifies caramelized flavors.

While the methods may vary in both traditional kopi roasting and specialty coffee, the focus remains on enhancing bold flavors or preserving delicate notes to craft the final coffee experience.

At Dutch Colony Coffee Co., we take roasting seriously because we know that every small detail makes a difference in the final cup. That's why we chose the Loring Kestrel S35, a modern roasting machine that gives us precise control over every stage of the roast. Unlike traditional drum roasters, which heat the beans through direct contact with the drum, the Loring uses convection heat with an air-recirculating system. This means the heat is distributed more evenly, allowing for better flavor clarity and consistency across batches.

One of the things we appreciate most about the Loring is its fuel efficiency. It reduces energy consumption by up to 80%, which helps lower emissions and makes the roasting process more sustainable. Knowing that we can roast incredible coffee while keeping our carbon footprint smaller is something we take pride in. Sustainability has always been important to us, and having equipment that aligns with our values makes the entire process even more meaningful.

Beyond its efficiency, what sets the Loring apart is the level of control it provides. We can fine-tune every aspect: temperature curves, airflow, and drum speed, to enhance the unique flavors of each batch. Whether it's a rich and nutty Guatemalan coffee or a smooth and caramel-like Colombian bean, this machine allows us to bring out the natural characteristics of each origin while ensuring a balanced and consistent roast every time.

I still remember the first time I worked on the Loring Kestrel S35. Standing in front of the machine, I felt both excited and a little nervous. The control panel, with its precise temperature settings, airflow adjustments, and rate-of-rise indicators, was completely different from the traditional drum roasters I was used to. Roasting had always been about intuition, reading the beans through sight, sound, and smell. Now, it was also about diving into the science of heat application, airflow dynamics, and how every single second could impact the final flavor.

As the first batch of green coffee beans poured into the roasting chamber, I watched them spin in a controlled vortex of hot air. The heat surrounded them evenly, unlike the direct contact of a traditional drum roaster. I listened closely, waiting for the first crack—the moment when the beans expand and release an audible pop, marking a critical stage in their development. The beans shifted in color, starting as pale green, turning golden brown, and finally deepening into rich caramel hues. I took a deep breath, savoring the changing aromas. At first, they were grassy and raw, but then they grew sweet and nutty as the sugars caramelized.

Even with all the technology available, I quickly learned that roasting is still an art that combines scientific precision with sensory awareness. You listen for the first crack, watch the beans shift in color, and take in the changing aromas, fully aware that every second counts. A split-second decision can mean the difference between a coffee that sings with bright citrusy notes and one that turns out flat or overdeveloped.

Every coffee variety responds differently to heat. A light roast preserves delicate floral and fruity notes, making it ideal for Ethiopian and Kenyan coffees. A medium roast creates a balance of acidity and sweetness, bringing out caramel and chocolate undertones. Darker roasts develop deep, bold flavors with a heavier body, often preferred for espresso blends. The challenge lies in knowing how each bean reacts, as some need a slow, steady heat to highlight their complexity, while others require a more aggressive approach to unlock their full potential.

Working on the Loring that day, I felt a deep respect for the delicate balance between science and intuition. The machine gives us the technical control to be precise, but at the end of the day, it's the roaster's instincts, experience, and passion that make the difference. Whether it's crafting a single-origin coffee that highlights the terroir of a farm or curating a blend that balances different flavor notes, every batch that comes out of our roastery is a reflection of this balance.

This is why I always remind myself that roasting is a journey. It's about pushing boundaries to unlock the unique potential of every bean and refining our process to create something exceptional. Each roast carries a story, an experience, and a lesson that builds toward something greater. I'll be sure to reflect on this and share a key snippet of my story with you when this chapter closes.

The Singapore Coffee Association

Beyond the journey of a coffee bean, I want to shed some light on the Singapore Coffee Association (SCA) and the role it plays in shaping the local industry. My first real encounter with the organization was in 2009, and to say it was unexpected would be an understatement.

At the time, I was organizing a barista competition through my Facebook group, I Am A Barista In Singapore. It wasn't backed by any major sponsors or official institutions. It was purely driven by passion, by the belief that Singapore needed a platform for baristas to showcase their skills and push the boundaries of what was possible in coffee.

I had envisioned an event that would bring baristas together, building healthy competition and camaraderie. But what I didn't realize was that, in doing so, I had unknowingly stepped into the jurisdiction of the Singapore Coffee Association. A warning came swiftly.

I was told in no uncertain terms that using the Barista Championship namesake without proper authorization could lead to legal action. It caught me off guard. I had never intended to challenge any governing body. In my mind, I was simply creating an opportunity for baristas. But in the eyes of the association, this was official territory, and I had crossed a line.

At the event, two figures stood out in the crowd: the President and Vice President of the SCA. They didn't step in or shut the event down, but their presence was enough to send a clear message. This wasn't just an underground barista gathering anymore. It had attracted attention from the people who oversaw Singapore's coffee industry at an institutional level.

The warning could have been discouraging, but instead, it became a moment of realization. If I truly wanted to make an impact, I needed to understand the structures that existed, the organizations that shaped policies, and the ecosystem that governed coffee in Singapore. Passion alone wasn't enough. I had to find a way to work within the system if I wanted to help change it.

And for the record, I renamed the competition. What had originally been planned under the Barista Championship name became the Cuppa-Barista Challenge: the same competition, the same mission, just with a different name.

After the event, I took a step back and reassessed my approach. Instead of running competitions on my own, I chose to immerse myself in the system. I decided to compete in an officially sanctioned Singapore Coffee Association (SCA) event, experiencing firsthand what it meant to work within the established framework of the industry.

It was a shift from organizing an independent competition to stepping into a structured arena where every rule, every detail, and every performance was measured against global coffee standards. Competing in an official setting gave me an entirely new perspective, one that helped me see why these structures existed and how they contributed to the larger coffee movement.

Over time, I became more involved, transitioning into a role within the unofficial barista guild. This allowed me to see how the association operated from the inside, including the challenges they faced, the influence they held, and the impact they had on shaping Singapore's coffee scene.

The Singapore Coffee Association (SCA) has long been the backbone of the nation's specialty coffee movement. Established to promote and develop Singapore's coffee industry, it serves as a bridge between farmers, roasters, baristas, and café owners, nurturing collaboration and education at every level.

One of its most significant contributions has been organizing national-level barista competitions, providing a platform for local talent to refine their craft, gain recognition, and compete on the world stage. Beyond competitions, the SCA plays a crucial role in advocacy. It helps shape policies that impact coffee businesses, works toward fair trade practices, and supports sustainability initiatives that benefit not only local café owners but also the global coffee supply chain.

Education and training have become additional pillars of SCA's mission, equipping coffee professionals with globally recognized certifications that set industry standards. Through workshops, courses, and structured training programs, the SCA provides baristas, roasters, and café owners with the tools they need to refine their craft.

By aligning with international coffee organizations, the SCA ensures that Singapore remains a serious player in the global coffee industry. Looking back, my first encounter with the Singapore Coffee Association was a defining moment in my journey. What started as a conflict, a warning about unauthorized competition, eventually became an opportunity for learning, growth, and collaboration.

During my time serving in the organization, I never forgot the words of the Vice President:

"Do not ask what the organization can do for you or Singapore's coffee industry, but rather, what can you do for the SCA and the industry?"

It was a challenge to shift my perspective, to see beyond personal ambition and recognize the bigger picture. Coffee is bigger than any one person or business. It is an ecosystem, and the strength of that ecosystem depends on those willing to contribute to its growth.

Today, I have stepped back from an active role in the organization, but my connection to it remains. Every year, I continue to volunteer as a national judge, giving back in the same way that the competitions once shaped me. Dutch Colony also remains an active corporate member, supporting the industry in the way that so many before me have.

Keeping Coffee Safe and Sustainable

Besides competition and industry development, there is another important aspect of coffee that often goes unnoticed: food safety compliance. Behind every bag of freshly roasted coffee is a set of strict regulations that determine where and how coffee can be roasted, especially in Singapore.

Unlike in some countries where small-batch roasting inside a café is common, Singapore's food safety laws require a more structured approach. The Singapore Food Agency (SFA) has clear guidelines that separate retail coffee roasting from commercial distribution. If a café wants to roast coffee for its own use, it may be allowed under specific conditions. However, the moment a business decides to sell its roasted coffee to other cafés, restaurants, or retailers, it must relocate to a food-safe factory space that meets SFA's hygiene and safety requirements.

The reasoning behind this regulation is clear: food safety, air quality, and operational sustainability. Coffee roasting requires high temperatures, produces smoke, and releases volatile organic compounds, all of which, if not managed properly, can cause air pollution and fire hazards. Many café spaces are not equipped with proper smoke filtration and ventilation systems, which could create risks for public health and neighboring businesses. By requiring roasters to operate in factory-zoned areas, these regulations ensure that food safety protocols are followed, reducing the risk of contamination while maintaining consistent production standards.

But compliance in the coffee industry goes beyond where coffee is roasted. It also applies to importing, handling, and distribution. Singapore has some of the strictest food import regulations in the region, and businesses must go through licensing requirements, food safety audits, and quality assurance processes before their coffee reaches consumers. Running a coffee roastery means tackling multiple layers of compliance, from obtaining an SFA license for food processing to securing import permits for green beans. There are also environmental regulations in place to manage waste disposal and emissions, ensuring that businesses operate responsibly.

These regulations are necessary to protect consumers and uphold food safety, but they also add layers of complexity to running a coffee business. It requires careful planning, investment in infrastructure, and a commitment to maintaining high standards. For those of us in the industry, these challenges are part of the journey, pushing us to refine our processes, innovate where possible, and stay dedicated to delivering quality coffee in a responsible way.

Let me tell you about a challenge we faced firsthand in this context. When we first started roasting, we operated in a café setting, where we could be hands-on with every batch and see customer reactions in real-time. There was something special about having the roaster right there in the café. Customers could watch the process unfold, see the green beans tumbling into the drum, smell the caramelizing sugars as the roast developed, and hear the distinct first crack as the beans expanded. It gave them a sense of transparency and connection to the craft, reinforcing the idea that coffee was an experience.

But as Dutch Colony Coffee Co. grew, and we started supplying coffee to other businesses, we had to make a difficult transition. To comply with SFA regulations, we needed to move our roasting operations out of the café and into a factory space. It was a necessary step, but it wasn't an easy one.

Moving from a cozy, café-based roasting setup to an industrial space came with its own set of challenges. The biggest shift was the loss of customer interaction. We were used to engaging with people as they sipped their coffee, explaining the nuances of different roasts, and sharing our passion in real-time. In the factory, roasting became more structured and systematic. The environment was different, quieter, more isolated, and focused purely on production.

There were financial challenges too. Higher rental costs, increased utility bills, and the need for additional equipment meant that our operational expenses grew overnight. On top of that, productivity took a hit at first as adjusting to a larger space meant rethinking workflows, optimizing batch sizes, and managing inventory in a completely new way. What had once been second nature in a smaller setup now required careful planning and adaptation.

There were days when we questioned whether the move was worth it. We missed the warmth of the café, the immediacy of seeing a customer's reaction to a freshly roasted batch, and the direct engagement that had fueled our passion.

Over time, we began to see the bigger picture. Setting up a dedicated roastery in a factory zone gave us the ability to scale production efficiently. It let us keep up with growing demand from our wholesale clients without compromising the quality that we're known for. The larger space also gave us room to fine-tune our roasting process, streamline workflows, and improve storage for both green beans and roasted coffee.

One of the biggest advantages was the ability to install proper ventilation systems and invest in advanced equipment. In a café setting, managing smoke and air quality was always a challenge, but in a factory space, we had full control over these aspects.

The environment was cleaner, more controlled, and designed specifically for high-volume roasting, allowing us to maintain consistency across every batch.

Beyond operational efficiency, having a food-safe facility gave our wholesale customers peace of mind. They could trust that every batch of coffee was roasted under strict hygiene and safety standards, meeting both local and international food safety regulations. This trust meant a lot, especially for businesses relying on dependable suppliers to deliver high-quality coffee. This credibility led to bigger collaborations and partnerships, helping us grow in ways we never imagined when we first started.

Sustainability Beyond Compliance

While following food safety regulations is necessary, we see it as an opportunity to prioritize sustainability in every aspect of our operations. Roasting in a dedicated factory space with energy-efficient machines, like our Loring Kestrel S35, allows us to make choices that are better for both the environment and the quality of our coffee. The Loring's closed-loop system recirculates heat, cutting down fuel consumption and emissions compared to traditional drum roasters. Many older roasting setups require an afterburner to manage smoke, which burns extra fuel and increases environmental impact. The Loring eliminates this need, making our roasting process cleaner, more efficient, and far less wasteful.

This focus on sustainability takes the bigger picture into account. Across the world, the coffee industry is facing serious challenges: climate change, deforestation, and the economic struggles of farmers. Without proper support, many coffee-growing communities struggle to sustain their livelihoods. In Singapore, we've seen more coffee businesses take steps toward sustainability, whether through direct trade relationships with farmers, compostable packaging, or waste reduction initiatives.

At Dutch Colony, we've made conscious choices about where and how we source our coffee. We work closely with importers who uphold ethical sourcing standards, ensuring that the farmers behind our coffee are fairly paid and supported in their agricultural efforts.

We have also been exploring more sustainable packaging options to reduce waste and lessen our environmental footprint. Finding the right balance between functionality, freshness, and eco-friendliness has been a challenge, but it's one we are committed to tackling.

Looking back at our journey, it's clear that the decision to move into a factory setting was about building a coffee business that could withstand the test of time, one that meets food safety regulations, prioritizes sustainability, and delivers consistent quality at scale. Making this shift required difficult adjustments, but in the long run, it allowed us to grow, refine our craft, and gain credibility as a trusted roaster.

For any aspiring coffee roaster looking to establish a presence in Singapore and expand beyond a single café, this transition is a necessary step. The process comes with its own set of challenges, including higher costs, operational changes, and adapting to an industrial environment, but it also lays the foundation for long-term growth and sustainability. The ability to scale while maintaining quality and compliance is what sets a strong coffee business apart.

That said, stepping into a factory space is just one part of the bigger picture. I want to focus on some of the biggest challenges facing local roasters today, challenges that extend beyond this transition.

Challenges Facing Local Roasters

Even with the growing appreciation for specialty coffee in Singapore, local roasteries face steep challenges in an industry dominated by global coffee chains with massive marketing budgets and well-established supply chains. Competing with these brands is about finding ways to stand out, whether that's through unique blends, personalized service, or a strong brand identity. On top of all that, there's another challenge that's specific to Singapore and Southeast Asia as a whole—the deeply ingrained traditional kopi culture.

In Western countries and other developed Asian markets like Korea and Japan, specialty coffee has become the norm. In Singapore, however, the coffee culture remains deeply rooted in kopitiams. Kopi is a cultural staple and an affordable daily ritual that many Singaporeans have grown up with. For generations, people have visited kopitiams, ordered their kopi-C or kopi-O, and enjoyed a familiar, comforting brew. This experience is so ingrained in daily life that it makes it harder for specialty coffee, with its focus on high-quality arabica, light-to-medium roasts, and terroir-driven flavors, to gain widespread acceptance as the standard. This cultural gap is something every specialty roaster in Singapore has to tackle.

Another major challenge that specialty coffee roasters face in Singapore is price perception. Traditional kopi, made using robusta-heavy blends caramelized with sugar and margarine, is much cheaper than specialty coffee. A cup of kopi at a kopitiam typically costs under SGD $2, while a specialty brew starts at $5 or more. This price gap makes it hard to persuade mainstream consumers to switch, especially when many have grown up enjoying the bold, sweet, and full-bodied flavors of kopi.

Outside of kopitiams, cost-cutting is also a common practice in the commercial coffee industry. Many roasters focus on keeping prices low by using commodity-grade arabica, blending it with robusta, or even adding fillers like barley or maize. This allows them to provide businesses with cheaper coffee, prioritizing volume over quality. For specialty coffee roasters, this creates an extra challenge. We prioritize quality, traceability, and ethical sourcing, which naturally increase costs. Unlike large-scale roasters who focus on affordability, specialty roasters invest in direct trade relationships, higher-quality beans, and precise roasting techniques to bring out the best in every cup.

The truth is, specialty coffee still caters to a niche audience—people who understand and appreciate the difference. While the demand for high-quality, ethically sourced coffee is growing, it hasn't yet reached a level where it can compete profitably with traditional coffee. This leaves specialty roasters constantly balancing their commitment to quality with the challenge of making specialty coffee more accessible to a broader audience.

And then there's the challenge of setting up a roastery, a process that is far from simple. Beyond dealing with strict food safety regulations, which require businesses to roast in a food-safe factory instead of a café, the financial investment is considerable. A high-quality roasting machine, quality control tools, and proper packaging systems can quickly add up to hundreds of thousands of dollars. And that's without considering Singapore's high rental costs, the ongoing expense of sourcing green beans, and the challenge of finding wholesale clients who often prioritize price over quality. As I mentioned earlier, moving to a factory setting pushed us to rethink production, adapt to a less customer-facing environment, and find ways to scale while maintaining quality.

Aside from financial challenges, local roasters face the tricky task of balancing tradition with innovation. Singapore's coffee culture has long been defined by kopi, with its robusta-heavy blends, condensed milk, and traditional brewing methods passed down through generations. Meanwhile, the growing popularity of specialty coffee has brought in new techniques, flavors, and experiences, appealing to a different group of coffee enthusiasts.

How do you stay true to heritage while embracing modern trends? For many roasters, the answer is a mix of adaptation and education. Some bridge the gap by offering a varied menu, keeping kopi alive while introducing specialty blends that highlight the natural flavors of high-quality arabica. Others experiment with new techniques while respecting traditional coffee, refining roasting methods, improving sourcing practices, or creating drinks that honor both old and new influences.

To succeed in this space, storytelling is key. Consumers might hesitate to spend extra on a cup of specialty coffee, but when they learn about why certain beans cost more, how ethical sourcing supports farmers, and how roasting techniques shape flavor, they start to view coffee as more than just a caffeine boost. Education adds value beyond the price, giving local roasters a chance to build meaningful connections with their customers.

The journey to mainstream adoption might be slow, and the challenges are real, but the rising interest in specialty coffee shows something important: there is space for both tradition and innovation to thrive in Singapore's ever-evolving coffee culture.

As we've seen throughout this chapter, coffee is a craft, a commitment, and, for many of us, a way of life. Every stage, from sourcing beans to roasting them just right, from following strict regulations to making choices that support sustainability, requires patience, persistence, and a deep love for what we do.

Over the years, I've met people whose lives revolve around coffee in ways that go beyond just making a living. Farmers who wake before the sun, tending to their crops with care, knowing their hard work shapes the flavors we enjoy. Importers who travel across continents, working to ensure fair pay and ethical sourcing, so the people who grow the beans get the recognition they deserve. Roasters and baristas who pour their time, energy, and passion into every batch and every cup, determined to make each one better than the last. And business owners who push forward, even when profits are slim and the competition is tough, because walking away from coffee isn't an option; it's what they love, and that love keeps them going.

But love for coffee alone isn't enough. Mastery in this craft comes from making mistakes, feeling the pressure, and learning to adapt. The moment I had promised to share while we talked about roasting is one that has stayed with me for years. It was a lesson in humility, pressure, and resilience that I carry to this day.

It happened during my time at Toby's Estate, a time full of unexpected challenges that really pushed me to grow. Toby Smith, the founder of the company, had flown into Singapore for a visit, and there was a buzz of excitement in the roastery. That day, we were setting up a brand-new sample roaster, a process I knew like the back of my hand after doing it so many times. Roasting had become second nature to me, something I could do without overthinking. But for some reason, that day felt different.

Toby turned to me and said, "Fire it up, let's do a test roast."

The beans he handed me were decaf. Not the most exciting choice, but it still needed to be done right. I nodded, got into the usual flow, and started the process. But as I reached for the controls, I couldn't ignore Toby standing right behind me. He was watching every move, his presence so close I could feel the weight of his stare.

My hands, usually steady, felt off. My timing wavered. I found myself second-guessing everything I was doing. In my nervousness, I roasted the decaf far too dark. The beans turned oily, a clear sign of overdevelopment. I stood there, staring at them, knowing I had messed up. Toby looked at me and asked, "What do you think?"

I hesitated for a moment before answering honestly. "Boss, I've done this so many times before, but today, with you watching over my shoulder... I just wasn't comfortable."

His response was short, sharp, and unforgettable:

"Suhaimi, you are only as good as your last roast."

His words hit me hard. It didn't matter how many successful roasts I had done before that moment. It didn't matter how many times I had nailed the perfect profile, balanced the acidity, or brought out the subtle floral notes in a delicate Ethiopian bean. What mattered was the roast I had just ruined. That was the reality of this craft. Every batch, every roast, every cup was a reflection of where you stood at that moment. There was no space for complacency.

I carried that thought with me for the rest of the day, replaying every misstep of that failed roast in my head. I knew I'd let the pressure get to me, but I also knew I'd learned something valuable. It was about staying composed, trusting myself, and keeping steady even when the heat is on and someone's breathing down your neck.

Later that evening, once things had quieted down at the roastery, Toby turned to me and suggested we head to the bar next door for a drink. Amused by the fact that I didn't drink, he went to the bartender and ordered a ginger ale for himself. It was clear he was trying to make me feel comfortable.

We found a small table tucked away in the corner, away from the bustle of the room but close enough to feel part of the atmosphere. At first, we talked about coffee, about the roast profiles we had experimented with earlier that day, comparing notes on flavor and technique. We even debated the unfair reputation of decaf beans, laughing at how much skill actually goes into processing them, yet how often they're dismissed. But after a while, the conversation shifted.

Toby started sharing stories, peeling back the layers of his journey, revealing the sacrifices and struggles that had shaped him. He told me about the early days, when he packed coffee by hand in his father's garage. Back then, there were no high-tech packaging machines, no glossy branding, just brown kraft paper bags, a handwritten label, and his personal signature on every pack. He laughed as he recounted how he would spend hours making sure each detail was just right before delivering the bags himself to customers.

As the night wore on, he began to share the tougher parts of his journey: the endless, draining hours, the moments he missed with his family, and the constant stress of running a business in a cutthroat industry with razor-thin profit margins.

He talked about losing some of his best people, employees he had trained and nurtured, who eventually left for higher-paying jobs at bigger companies. The sting of that loss never really went away. He admitted there were moments when he thought about walking away, questioning whether it was all worth it. The constant pressure to scale, grow, and meet demand, all while holding onto the values he built his company on, weighed heavily on him.

There were easier ways to do business, like cutting costs by sourcing cheaper, non-specialty beans, speeding up production by compromising on quality, or following market trends instead of staying true to his own philosophy.

"But if I did that," he said, staring into his glass, "it wouldn't be the business I set out to build."

That conversation with Toby left me thinking long after I walked away from the bar that night. It reinforced something I had already felt deeply in my own journey: coffee is about people. It's about the hands that grow it, the minds that source and roast it, the baristas who bring it to life, and the communities that gather around it.

Ironically, Toby's Estate was also the last coffee company I worked for before fully stepping into my next chapter as a co-partner of Dutch Colony Coffee Co in 2014. In a way, my transition felt almost poetic. Just a year before taking that leap, I was still working as the Wholesale Manager at Toby's, supplying Dutch Colony with coffee and café essentials like chocolate, chai, and even espresso grinders. Some of those grinders still sit proudly in our academy today, silent reminders of the path that brought me here.

Looking back, it's impossible to ignore how the pieces came together. The road to Dutch Colony was never planned in precise steps, but somehow, it was inevitable. And if there's one thing I've learned from this industry, it's that coffee has a way of leading you exactly where you're meant to be.

CHAPTER 3

From Kopi to Cold Brew

If Starbucks was where I learned the science of coffee, Hui Yee Coffee was where I learned its soul. Moving from the polished efficiency of a global coffee chain to the heart of a family-run kopi business was both exciting and a bit daunting. Here, everything relied on intuition, muscle memory, and decades of tradition handed down through generations. No fancy machines or sleek espresso bars. Just well-worn roasting drums and kopi socks stained dark from years of brewing. It was raw, unfiltered, and proudly traditional. As I hinted in the earlier chapter, I was brought in to help modernize the brand, moving beyond just traditional kopi to something that embodies youthful energy, a progressive vision, and a wider gourmet range.

From 2007 to 2011, specialty coffee was still a quiet player in Singapore, barely making a dent in a market dominated by robusta-heavy kopi. But my boss, Alex Chong, saw the potential. He believed in innovation and staying ahead of the curve, which is why he gave me his full support to push boundaries. With his encouragement, I set up a coffee academy, opened a retail café and roastery, and even competed in barista championships to bring visibility to the company.

He understood that change was coming. But not everyone shared that vision. David Chong, his elder brother and the General Manager, saw things differently. For decades, he had built the company on tradition, roasting tonne after tonne of kopi beans, supplying countless kopitiams, and ensuring that the business thrived without ever needing to change. To him, what I was doing was an experiment at best. A passion project that, in his eyes, could never match the sheer volume, consistency, or profitability of their robusta trade.

His words still sit with me, sharp and unyielding: "How much can you even bring in from your 500kg to 800kg of gourmet business per month? Look at the tonnes of kopi we roast daily. The number of kopitiams we supply. What difference can you make?"

And then, there were the small, calculated jabs, casual enough to sound like instructions but pointed enough to remind me of my place.

"No, you roast it yourself after we're done with production." "You either start roasting before we begin for the day or you do it after we're finished."

There was no space for my project in the main schedule, no room in the system they had built. If I wanted to make this work, I had to do it on the fringes, outside of their structured, time-tested operation.

I wasn't broken by his words. If anything, they fueled me. If it meant waking up before dawn or staying back long after the machines had cooled, I was ready. If proving myself every single day was the price of being here, I would pay it willingly. I had learned early on that obstacles weren't meant to stop me. What stands in the way becomes the way.

But I also knew something else: arguing with David Chong wasn't going to change his mind. He had built this business on tradition, on years of perfecting a method that had stood the test of time. Words alone wouldn't convince him. I had to show him. So instead of resisting, I stepped into his world. I watched, I learned, and I made myself a part of the very thing I had come to challenge.

Every morning, I stood alongside the old-timers, tasting robusta after robusta, letting its deep bitterness and thick body settle on my tongue. I focused on the slight variations in flavor, the subtle differences between batches, and the way years of practice allowed the senior roasters to adjust heat levels without hesitation. I listened as they argued about bean density and roasting times, realizing that despite the resistance to change, there was an incredible amount of skill built into this craft.

I spent hours on the roasting floor, my hands following the same steps that had been practiced for decades: lifting sacks of raw green beans, measuring them with precision, and loading them into the roaring drum roaster. The smell of caramelizing sugar and margarine soaked into my clothes, a scent so deeply tied to kopi roasting that it became impossible to separate from the experience.

Then, the moment that changed everything arrived.

One morning, the usual hum of the roastery was missing. The workers were standing around in hushed conversation. Word spread quickly. There was a strike. The migrant workers responsible for daily production had walked out, refusing to work. Machines sat idle, orders piled up, and for the first time, no one was at the controls. The business had come to a halt.

No one knew what to do. This wasn't my responsibility; I wasn't in charge of kopi production. But I knew I had to step up. Without a second thought, I gathered my small team from the gourmet department. We weren't trained for this, and no one expected us to take over. But we did. We worked quickly, dividing tasks and stepping into roles we'd never officially held before. The heat from the roasting machines felt more intense that day, and the air was heavy with the weight of responsibility. We measured, roasted, and packed, making sure the supply chain didn't falter. Customers counting on their daily deliveries wouldn't be left waiting.

That was the turning point.

For the first time, David Chong didn't look at us as outsiders trying to push an unfamiliar agenda. He saw us as people who were willing to carry the weight of the business alongside him. We weren't there to erase what had been built; we were there to evolve with it.

The invisible wall between us, the one that had kept tradition and innovation at odds, began to crumble. He never said it outright, but I could sense it in the way he observed us that day. There was a quiet acknowledgment, a recognition that we were here with action. And in a business like his, action was what counted.

That experience made me realize that specialty coffee wasn't just up against commercial chains with bigger marketing budgets.

The challenge ran deeper than that. It had to fight for space in the hearts and minds of those who had carried this industry long before "specialty coffee" was even a concept. It had to carve out its own place in a culture where coffee wasn't something new—it was an institution. And that fight wasn't won by pushing harder or talking louder. It was won through understanding.

This experience also reinforced something I had come to understand over the years: my journey in coffee has always been about bridging worlds. From the robust, caramelized depths of traditional kopi to the bright, intricate flavors of specialty coffee, I found myself constantly moving between two different but deeply rooted cultures.

If you had asked me in the early 2000s whether Singapore would one day be home to a thriving specialty coffee scene, I might have hesitated. There was no conversation about tasting notes, brew ratios, or single-origin beans. Coffee was functional, a necessity, not an experience. But change was brewing.

For decades, kopi stayed the same, with brewing techniques handed down through generations. Kopitiam culture flourished, and traditional coffee stalls became a key part of Singapore's identity. However, in the late 1990s and early 2000s, the coffee scene began to change as global coffee chains entered the market, offering a new way to enjoy coffee.

Starbucks led the way in this shift. When it came to Singapore, it transformed the way people thought about coffee. The chain brought premium Arabica beans to a market that had long been dominated by robusta-heavy kopi. With customizable drinks, modern interiors, curated music playlists, and free Wi-Fi, they created an environment that felt fresh and aspirational.

Unlike kopitiams, which focused on efficiency, Starbucks invited customers to stay and linger.

Coffee, which had long been a simple morning staple, was now tied to identity. For many young professionals and students in Singapore, visiting Starbucks or similar chains became an experience, a ritual, and at times, a quiet status symbol. Holding a branded takeaway cup felt like being part of something bigger, a connection to a cosmopolitan culture that was rapidly shaping the way people lived, worked, and socialized.

Starbucks was not alone in fueling this transformation. Coffee Bean & Tea Leaf, Spinelli, and other international chains carved out their own space, each offering a different take on what a café could be. They were spaces to meet friends, finish assignments, hold casual business meetings, or simply escape the demands of a fast-moving city. The appeal was undeniable.

When the World Meets the Cup

With the rise of specialty coffee, Singapore did not simply follow Western trends. The coffee culture began to absorb influences from all over Asia, blending tradition with innovation while still retaining its own unique identity. I have witnessed this transformation myself.

One strong influence comes from Japan, where coffee is treated as an art of precision and simplicity. Japanese coffee culture values craftsmanship, patience, and ritual. The slow coffee movement in Japan focuses on techniques like pour-over, siphon brewing, and hand-drip methods, all of which require careful attention and respect for each ingredient. In traditional

Japanese coffeehouses, known as kissaten, every cup is served with a calm and deliberate focus, allowing the flavors to truly shine.

Singapore has taken these ideas to heart. At Nylon Coffee Roasters, a pioneer in the specialty coffee scene, the Japanese philosophy of small-batch roasting is alive and well, with a focus on achieving clarity and balance in every cup. Apartment Coffee offers a tranquil experience similar to a Japanese kissaten, featuring minimalist interiors, a straightforward menu, and an emphasis on pure, clean flavors. Even at Dutch Colony Coffee Co., the art of slow coffee is celebrated through single-origin pour-over bars, where the selections rotate monthly. This approach allows customers to explore and appreciate the subtle differences between beans, much like in Japan's third-wave cafés. Another example that stands out to me is the growing popularity of kopi-inspired specialty drinks, such as the "dirty coffee." Originally from Japan, this drink has spread across Asia and features a shot of hot espresso poured over cold milk, creating a bold yet creamy layered effect. Another highlight is the Gula Melaka latte, which mixes the rich, caramelized sweetness of palm sugar with espresso and milk for a uniquely Southeast Asian twist on specialty coffee.

While Japan's influence on Singapore's coffee culture is rooted in precision and ritual, South Korea has shaped a different side of the experience. Korean cafés are designed to be destinations where people can hang out, take photos, and socialize. Whether it's sleek, modern spaces with artistic furniture or cozy themed setups that feel like stepping into an art gallery, Korean coffee culture beautifully mixes coffee with design, fashion, and social media charm.

Singapore has embraced this concept in its own way. Cafés like Equate Coffee and Kreams Krafthouse showcase Korean-inspired interiors, featuring neutral tones, clean lines, and soft lighting that create a cozy and welcoming vibe. South Korea's influence doesn't stop at design—it has also shaped home brewing trends. The Dalgona coffee craze, which went viral during the pandemic, originated in South Korea and quickly became a favorite among Singaporeans trying out coffee-making at home. Even café menus reflect this influence, with coffee often paired with eye-catching desserts like soufflé pancakes and bingsu served with espresso. This combination blends the indulgence of Korean-inspired treats with Singapore's growing appreciation for specialty coffee.

The influences from Thailand and Malaysia introduced something unique, representing an evolution of heritage. Both countries have found a way to modernize their traditional coffee while preserving the essence that makes it so special. In Thailand, coffee has always been closely tied to local flavors. A classic example is Thai iced coffee, or Oliang, a strong brew mixed with condensed milk and often spiced with cardamom or star anise. Even as third-wave coffee gained popularity, Thai cafés managed to honor their roots. Drinks featuring coconut, pandan, and Thai tea-infused coffee became favorites, combining traditional Southeast Asian ingredients with modern brewing methods. This blend of tradition and innovation has also shaped how specialty coffee is crafted in Singapore, inspiring the use of local flavors in modern coffee menus.

Malaysia has managed to hold onto its kopi culture while also making room for specialty coffee. Traditional kopitiams are still a key part of daily life, but third-wave cafés are finding ways to blend Nanyang coffee elements into modern coffee experiences. Perhaps the most exciting shift is the rise of Nanyang-style specialty coffee, where robusta beans, long associated with kopitiams, are now being treated with specialty-grade precision. Instead of the usual high-heat caramelization, some roasters are using modern roasting techniques to highlight the natural complexity of these beans. This creates a bridge between Singapore's kopi heritage and the growing specialty coffee scene.

Singapore, being a melting pot of cultures, has taken all these influences and done something remarkable; it has made them its own. Instead of choosing between tradition and innovation, it has found a way to embrace both, creating a coffee culture that is uniquely Singaporean. This is a city where the deep caramelized notes of kopi sit comfortably alongside the bright acidity of single-origin espresso.

Some cafés have fully embraced this duality, offering both traditional kopi and specialty coffee under one roof. Places like Coffee Break have redefined a kopitiam, serving nostalgic brews made with robusta while also experimenting with specialty-grade beans and alternative brewing methods.

This blend of old and new is also reflected in menus that have evolved to include drinks inspired by both kopitiam heritage and third-wave coffee. Locally inspired creations such as kopi lattes, ondeh-ondeh cold brews, and salted egg yolk mochas have become part of the scene, merging global trends with flavors that Singaporeans recognize and love.

Even traditional kopitiam chains have taken steps to modernize. Brands like Ya Kun Kaya Toast and Toast Box have given kopi a more polished experience, with stylish interiors, streamlined self-service kiosks, and a café-style atmosphere. While the brewing techniques remain largely the same, the presentation and customer experience have evolved, making traditional kopi feel accessible to younger generations who might otherwise gravitate toward international coffee chains.

This shift has sparked a new wave among coffee drinkers in Singapore. I've noticed many young consumers start their mornings with a familiar cup of kopi for that nostalgic kick, then later in the day, they switch to specialty coffee to enjoy its subtle, layered flavors. Some alternate between the two, depending on their mood or the occasion, and it's clear that the love for both styles is growing.

This blending of cultures can also be seen in Singapore's coffee events, where traditional kopi and specialty coffee come together in the same space. Festivals like the Singapore Coffee Festival (SCF) celebrate the entire coffee spectrum, from the thick, caramelized richness of traditional kopi to the bright, fruity flavors of a natural-processed Ethiopian brew. At these events, I've watched local roasters experiment with kopi-inspired specialty drinks, using high-quality robusta beans roasted with the same precision as single-origin arabica. It's an exciting fusion of techniques, where specialty coffee draws from tradition rather than replacing it.

At the crux of this evolution, we at Dutch Colony Coffee Co. played a key role in shaping Singapore's café brunch culture. We took inspiration from Australia's lively brunch scene and were among the early pioneers to blend specialty coffee with an all-day brunch menu. In our cafés, coffee became a centerpiece for weekend gatherings, work meetings, and casual catch-ups. Much like Industry Beans in Melbourne or Common Man Coffee Roasters in Singapore, we built our reputation by serving excellent coffee alongside a carefully designed food program that enhances the entire experience.

I also observed how Nylon Coffee Roasters made its mark by forging direct trade relationships with farmers. In the early days of Singapore's specialty coffee movement, this approach was rare. They worked closely with producers to ensure ethical sourcing while maintaining high quality. This commitment to fair practices and traceability showed that a great cup of coffee is built on respect and care at every step, from the farm to the final brew.

Additionally, Alchemist Coffee transformed quick-service specialty coffee by mastering the grab-and-go concept with sleek, minimalist kiosks that serve high-quality coffee to busy urban professionals. It brought to mind places like Omotesando Koffee in Japan, % Arabica in Hong Kong, and Blue Bottle in Korea. These brands showed that takeaway coffee can be quick and still taste great, making specialty coffee easier to enjoy for busy commuters.

Meanwhile, innovative cafés like Atlas Coffeehouse and Brawn & Brains started to redefine the café experience. They introduced Instagram-worthy brunch plates alongside carefully crafted specialty coffee, a concept reminiscent of the aesthetic approach seen at % Arabica Kyoto and Fritz Coffee Company in Seoul.

Today, stepping into a café in Singapore means encountering a nuanced blend of global influences. A single coffeehouse might serve an artisanal pour-over inspired by Japanese kissaten culture, feature a space designed with Seoul's sleek coffee vibes, or offer a reimagined kopi infused with flavors from Singapore's heritage. This diversity has turned Singapore into a coffee tourism hotspot, where visitors hunt for unique café experiences just as they do with food. Across Asia, this trend has gained momentum. Hidden micro-roasteries in Bangkok and Kuala Lumpur focus on regional beans, while in Seoul, cafés offer immersive experiences. These range from hanok-inspired traditional spaces to futuristic concept bars. In Bangkok, spots like Factory Coffee and Roots Coffee Roasters showcase Southeast Asian beans, proving that exceptional coffee isn't limited to origins like Ethiopia or Colombia.

Brewing the Evolution: Kopi to Gourmet to Specialty

While this evolution and growth might seem like it happened overnight, the reality is that it was a gradual transition. Reflecting on the early days, I remember Hui Yee, which I talked about in the beginning of this chapter. Back then, I was the one who led its transformation into Cuppachoice with the support and vision of my boss, Alex Chong. We started out with traditional kopi, brewing coffee the same way it had been for generations. Over time, we noticed a growing demand for gourmet coffee, something that could bridge the gap between the familiar robusta blends of traditional kopi and the emerging world of specialty coffee.

We began introducing higher-quality arabica beans and experimenting with new roasting profiles. Our focus shifted from merely delivering strong and efficient coffee to creating drinks that celebrated flavor and experience. The change was not easy. There was skepticism and resistance from those who believed tradition should remain untouched like David Chong, the general manager, and we faced the constant challenge of proving that this shift was not a passing trend but a meaningful evolution.

In those days, every new batch was a lesson. I learned to balance the old with the new, to respect the legacy of traditional kopi while exploring fresh ways to bring out the nuances of quality beans.

Yet, we weren't alone in this journey. Between 2008 and 2010, a few pioneers took bold steps to bring specialty coffee to Singapore. I remember when Oriole Coffee Roasters opened in 2008, founded by Keith Loh. It was one of the first specialty roasters in the city, and it played a major role in introducing barista culture and coffee competitions. It became a meeting place where early coffee professionals, including myself, would share ideas and learn from one another.

In 2009, Papa Palheta, now known as PPP Coffee, was co-founded by Leon Foo. This venture introduced a "cafe-within-a-roastery" concept. By challenging the idea that specialty coffee had to be slow, expensive, or impractical for busy professionals, it provided customers with access to single-origin coffees and expertly crafted espresso drinks.

These brands led a transformation, bringing traceable coffee origins, alternative brewing methods, and a greater appreciation for coffee as something more than just a morning ritual. Their efforts weren't happening in a vacuum. Across Asia, similar movements were emerging in cities like Tokyo, Bangkok, and Seoul as the demand for coffee continued to grow.

Amidst this story of transformation, I want to take a step back and share a personal moment that shaped my journey. Before I fully embraced specialty coffee, my world revolved around robusta and commercial-grade arabica. Coffee, at the time, was about efficiency, boldness, and strength. It wasn't about delicate flavors, terroir, or nuanced tasting notes. The goal was to produce a consistent, full-bodied brew that satisfied the local demand.

That perspective changed dramatically in 2008 when I attended a competition barista workshop led by New Zealand barista champion Carl Sara. I didn't know what to expect, but I remember being curious enough to step outside of my comfort zone and listen to someone who had a completely different approach to coffee. During the workshop, I took a sip of coffee that made me stop in my tracks. It wasn't bitter. It wasn't just strong. It had an intense, almost shocking burst of flavor. Blueberries. Not subtle hints, but an unmistakable, juicy, fruit-forward profile that was unlike anything I had tasted before. And when paired with milk, it transformed into something entirely new, similar to a blueberry milkshake or even a bowl of Froot Loops soaked in milk. It was coffee, but at the same time, it was something else entirely.

That sip stayed with me long after the workshop ended. It planted a seed in my mind, one that grew over the next year as I started questioning everything I thought I knew about coffee. Then, in 2009, during the opening of our café, I received a gift from Young In, a respected green bean importer in Singapore. He handed me a batch of Panama Gesha, a variety I had never roasted before. I wasn't sure what to expect, but as the beans roasted, an aroma filled the air that sent me straight back to that moment in Carl Sara's workshop. Floral, tea-like notes. A light, almost ethereal fruitiness.

That was the moment it all came full circle. This was my own journey, one that had started in the depths of traditional kopi roasting and had now brought me to a new world of specialty coffee that I was just beginning to understand.

My journey from gourmet coffee to specialty coffee also played out on the competitive stage. In my final years at Starbucks in 2007, I took part in the Coffee Ambassador Championship and came out on top. For my final presentation, I wanted to do something that paid homage to my roots. I brewed a Sumatra Mandheling using a French press, but instead of serving it in a typical café cup, I poured it into a traditional tin milk can, the kind used in kopitiams for condensed milk. I punched a hole in the lid and threaded a raffia string through it, just like the makeshift takeaway cups of the past. Beside it, I placed a small serving of condensed milk, allowing the judges to experience the coffee the way many Singaporeans, including my Atuk and Ayah, had enjoyed it for generations: strong, bold, and steeped in nostalgia.

This bridging of two coffee cultures, finding ways to honor tradition while embracing change, was an instinct then, but it became a philosophy that shaped my journey in the years to come.

When I left Starbucks and stepped into the world of traditional kopi, my perspective on coffee shifted once again. Instead of working with espresso machines and Arabica beans, I found myself roasting robusta, diving into the details of caramelization, and learning about the economics of large-scale coffee production. Even as I became deeply involved in kopi, I was aware that coffee culture was continuing to evolve, and I wanted to evolve with it.

I watched my first Barista Championship in 2008, mesmerized by the level of precision and storytelling that went into every performance. It was a completely different world from the fast-paced, high-volume environments I was used to. By 2009, I stepped onto the stage as a competitor for the first time. I had prepared for months, refining my technique and practicing my routine. But when the moment came, I lost track of time and exceeded the time limit, resulting in an automatic disqualification. It was a crushing blow. But I wasn't going to walk away. I had come too far, and I knew that this was just the beginning.

In 2010, I stepped back onto the competition stage with a newfound clarity. This time, I presented a blend of Brazilian and Ethiopian Arabica, balancing the chocolatey, nutty sweetness of Brazil with the bright, floral notes of Ethiopia. It paid off. I secured third place.

But I wasn't done. By 2011, I took another leap forward. Instead of blending origins, I made a bold decision to showcase a single coffee. I chose a Hawaiian coffee from Kau Forest, sourced from Malian Lahey, a female coffee farmer whose dedication to her craft inspired me.. I had moved beyond thinking of coffee as just taste or technique. I had begun to see the people behind it, their labor, their commitment, and the stories carried in every cup.

These competitions were never simply about winning for me. They mirrored my own growth and reflected how my view of coffee kept shifting, just as the local coffee culture was changing.

The journey through these competitions, from my first steps in 2009 to my role as a world-calibrated judge in recent years, is something I hold close to my heart. There's much to be said about this road from standing behind an espresso machine to standing behind the judge's table, and the lessons learned in between. But for now, I return to the present, to the very streets where my coffee journey began.

When I walk into a kopitiam, the smell of roasted robusta and evaporated milk fills the place, full of nostalgia. At a corner table, an elderly uncle sips his kopi O siew dai, his fingers wrapped around the glass mug, his gaze fixed on the morning paper. This is his ritual, one he has followed for decades.

A few streets away, a young barista stands behind the polished counter of a specialty café, carefully pouring hot water over freshly ground Ethiopian beans. The floral aroma rises from the V60 dripper as he watches the bloom, timing each pour with precision. He sets the cup down in front of a customer, offering a quiet nod, knowing that the coffee will speak for itself.

This contrast has never felt like a divide to me. Instead, it captures where Singapore's coffee culture stands today: a place where the past and future coexist, where nostalgia blends with innovation, and where no single definition of coffee dominates. And as long as there are people who are curious, passionate, and eager to explore both worlds, this story will continue to be written.

CHAPTER 4

Beyond the Cup – The Rise of Specialty Coffee

When I think about the rise of specialty coffee in Singapore, I am reminded of the puzzle pieces I used to fit together as a boy, sitting cross-legged on the floor beside my Ayah. He would sip his kopi, his fingers curled around the thick porcelain cup, while I studied the scattered pieces in front of me, trying to make sense of the bigger picture. Some pieces clicked into place easily, while others took longer to find their fit. But with each piece that connected, the image became clearer.

Specialty coffee, much like those puzzles, didn't arrive in Singapore all at once. It came together in fragments: small moments, individual efforts, and subtle shifts that slowly formed something bigger. And just like those puzzle sessions with Ayah, where I would glance up to see him watching me, letting me struggle a little before nudging me in the right direction, my own journey in this changing scene unfolded in much the same way.

Every experience added a layer of understanding. Competing in the Singapore National Barista Championship, watching the world's best baristas on livestream, standing backstage at the

World Barista Championship (WBC), and stealing sips from the rimmed ceramic cups left on competitors' carts—all of it shaped the way I saw coffee. I didn't always realize it at the time, but these moments weren't just competitions or fleeting encounters with great coffee. They were the puzzle pieces clicking into place and revealing a new world beyond kopi, beyond commercial espresso chains, and beyond what I had known.

But there was one afternoon in 2009 that changed everything for me. It was a before-and-after moment, like someone switching on a light in a darkened room. I had gone to a modest shophouse in Bukit Timah to meet the team at Papa Palheta, a leading specialty coffee boutique. At the time, I was both selling Cafelat barista accessories and discussing KeepCups, which they had recently started stocking. It was meant to be a straightforward visit, nothing out of the ordinary. But from the moment I stepped inside, something about the space caught me off guard. It wasn't a traditional café with elaborate menu boards, cash registers, or hurried transactions. Instead, it was a quiet, almost meditative environment where everything felt intentional.

The space was filled with the rich, unmistakable fragrance of freshly ground beans, but there was something else I couldn't quite place. It wasn't just the aroma that made the space feel unique. It was the way the baristas moved and spoke about coffee with an almost reverent attention. That afternoon, they placed a tall carafe in front of me, wrapped in a bandanna cloth. Inside was a washed single-origin coffee, something I had never tried before. There was no sugar or milk, just coffee served in a Duralex glass. The glass surprised me. I was used to ceramic mugs, their sturdy weight and the way they held heat. This glass, though, was smooth and light in my hand, its clarity reflecting the clarity of the moment.

I lifted it to my lips, took a sip, and for the first time, coffee didn't just taste like coffee. It was crisp and clean, with a brightness and balance I had never experienced before. The flavors revealed themselves gradually, subtle, delicate, and complex. I sat there, glass in hand, trying to process what had just happened. I had spent years around coffee, roasting it, brewing it, serving it. And yet, in this quiet shophouse, with one sip from a simple glass, I realized I had barely scratched the surface. That was the moment of clarity.

I couldn't shake the feeling as I made my way back to Hui Yee Coffee, now rebranded as Cuppachoice's main roastery in Bukit Batok. It had been some time since I last visited. After opening our café and retail space in Chinatown, where I operated the smaller 5kg Has Garanti roasting machine, most of my days had been spent there. The Bukit Batok roastery, where the much larger 60kg Has Garanti stood, felt distant in comparison. However, something about that afternoon at Papa Palheta made me feel the need to return, both physically and mentally.

When I arrived, the familiar scent of freshly roasted beans filled the atmosphere, thick and heavy, clinging to the walls and floors like an old memory.I walked past the burlap sacks of robusta and commercial-grade arabica and past the production team who were moving with steady efficiency, filling bags, sealing them, and stacking them. It was a world I knew intimately, yet somehow, after that experience at Papa Palheta, it felt like I was seeing it for the first time.

I met with my boss, Alex, in his office. The sounds of the roasters in the background were a constant, steady reminder of the work going on just outside. I wasted no time sharing what I had experienced that day: the clarity of the coffee, the way it had been served, the philosophy behind it all. There was an urgency in my voice, a need to put into words something that had hit me on a deeper level.

Alex listened, arms folded, nodding slightly as I spoke. Then, with a small smile, he leaned back and said, "Do you not remember Leon Foo?"

I frowned, the name familiar but distant.

"Leon Foo," Alex repeated. "The guy behind Papa Palheta. He was here at our roastery back in 2008. Uncle Tan from Tiong Hoe Coffee brought him in for a tour."

I couldn’t help but smile at the mention of Uncle Tan. He had been a fixture at the roastery, always working with precision, roasting big batches of fragrant Arabica beans with the kind of quiet confidence that only came from years of experience. There were days when I would stand beside him, watching the beans shift in color, listening for the first crack, and absorbing everything he shared. Those one-on-one roasting sessions had been some of the most valuable moments in my early career, providing an education far beyond what any book or training manual could offer.

Hearing Alex talk about Leon Foo and recalling how Papa Palheta had grown so quickly made me reflect on where we stood at Cuppachoice. Just a year earlier, Leon had been at our roastery as a visitor, and now, he was leading one of the most talked-about specialty coffee concepts in Singapore. In contrast, we were still finding our footing, caught between the past and the future, trying to balance our roots in traditional kopi with the possibilities of something new.

That moment made me question what I was building and whether I was growing in the right direction. I had spent years learning, adapting, and refining my craft, but standing still was never an option. If I truly wanted to push myself, to understand specialty coffee at a closer level and fully experience a culture where it had already flourished, I knew I had to take a leap.

Just two years later, I did. I bid my farewell to Cuppachoice and joined the 'Godfather' of specialty coffee in Australia, Toby's Estate. Founded in 1997, Toby's had carved out a reputation for excellence in Sydney and Melbourne. When they arrived in Singapore in 2011, it marked a shift in the local coffee scene. Their flagship café in the city quickly became a gathering place for coffee enthusiasts. People came to experience something different, and the café was filled with conversations about beans, roasting techniques, and brewing methods.

The Rise of Third-Wave Coffee in Singapore

As I immersed myself in this new chapter, I realized that Singapore's coffee culture was evolving in parallel. What was once a daily habit, a quick cup of kopi at a hawker stall or a grab-and-go latte from a chain, was beginning to transform into something more deliberate. People were starting to engage with coffee differently. They were tasting it, discussing it, seeking out specific origins, and learning about different brewing methods. Coffee was becoming a ritual and an experience to savor.

This shift mirrored a larger movement happening across the global coffee scene, one that had been gaining momentum for years: the rise of third-wave coffee. The term third-wave coffee came about as a way to address the limitations of the first and second waves of coffee. The first wave, which dominated much of the 20th century, was all about convenience and accessibility. Brands like Folgers and Maxwell House made coffee widely available, but with little regard for quality, origin, or flavor complexity. It was coffee in its most basic form: pre-ground, mass-produced, and functional.

The second wave, which gained traction in the 1960s and 1970s, brought with it a more refined appreciation for coffee. Brands like Peet's Coffee and Starbucks introduced espresso-based drinks to a global audience, along with the idea that coffee could have distinct origins. Consumers became familiar with terms like Colombian or Sumatra, but the focus was still largely on consistency, often favoring dark roasts that masked many of the beans' subtler characteristics.

And then, quietly at first but steadily growing, came the third wave that changed everything. It was driven by roasters, baristas, and consumers who wanted more: more transparency, more flavor, more connection to the farmers who grew the beans. This was when coffee stopped being just a product and became a craft that required skill, knowledge, and an appreciation for every step of the process, from farm to cup.

Singapore, like many other cities, was catching on to this shift. Specialty roasters were emerging, cafés were focusing on direct trade and traceability, and consumers were beginning to ask questions: Where is this coffee from? How was it processed? What flavors should I expect? The idea that coffee could be as complex as wine, with layers of tasting notes that reflected its origin, was no longer reserved for a niche group of enthusiasts. It was starting to take root in the mainstream.

So, in a nutshell, third-wave coffee signified a shift from mass-produced, generic coffee to a focus on quality, traceability, and craftsmanship. Every step, from selecting the right beans to roasting with precision and brewing with care, was designed to highlight the coffee's natural flavors rather than mask them.

This approach gave rise to single-origin beans and lighter roasts. For years, most people were used to darker, stronger coffees that focused on familiarity and boldness. Big coffee chains built their success on blends made for consistency, often roasting darker to keep the flavor uniform. Third-wave coffee introduced something completely different. Instead of blending beans to create a predictable profile, it celebrated the natural diversity of coffee, recognizing that beans from different regions carried distinct characteristics shaped by altitude, soil, and climate.

Common Man Coffee Roasters was one of the pioneers in Singapore leading this shift. Their focus wasn't just on serving great coffee, but on helping people understand why it mattered. They worked directly with farms to guarantee traceability and ethical sourcing, making sure every cup of coffee had a story. When customers stepped into their cafés, they were actively learning about the origins of their coffee, the farmers who grew the beans, and the conditions that influenced the flavors in their cup.

For many Singaporeans, this was their first experience with coffee that had hints of citrus, berries, or floral undertones, rather than the usual bitterness they were used to. It changed how people viewed coffee, showing that it could deliver depth, complexity, and craftsmanship in ways they had never imagined.

As the taste and appreciation for specialty coffee grew, so did the methods used to brew it. Instead of the mass-produced espresso shots from chain cafés or the quick kopi pulls of the kopitiams, alternative brewing methods like pour-over, AeroPress, and siphon brewing started gaining traction in local specialty cafés. These methods required patience and skill, offering baristas more control over extraction and allowing the unique characteristics of each coffee to shine.

The pour-over method, in particular, became a defining symbol of the craft behind specialty coffee. At Nylon Coffee Roasters, I would often see Dennis and Jia Min standing behind the brew bar, pouring hot water in slow, controlled circles over freshly ground coffee. The process was methodical, almost meditative, coaxing out delicate floral and fruity notes that would have otherwise been lost in traditional brewing methods. There was something deeply satisfying about watching this, an experience that stood in stark contrast to the automated machines of commercial coffee shops.

Perhaps the most noticeable transformation, though, was in the way people approached coffee. A growing segment of coffee drinkers in Singapore started seeking out cafés for the ritual of drinking it. Specialty cafés became spaces where people lingered, where conversations unraveled over a slow brew, and where coffee became a moment of pause. This shift in mindset was evident in cafés like Stranger's Reunion, which cultivated an environment where coffee was presented with the same care as a fine meal. Every detail, from the hand-selected beans to the choice of serving ware, was curated to enhance the drinking experience.

This growing appreciation for coffee was also shaped by international exposure. For many, their first true introduction to specialty coffee didn't happen within the walls of a local café. It happened in the alleys of Melbourne, where flat whites were served with a quiet confidence. It unfolded in the hidden kissaten of Tokyo, where baristas moved with the skill of craftsmen. It was discovered in the airy, minimalist coffee bars of Scandinavia, where light roasts were celebrated for their delicate, tea-like qualities. Travelers returning from these coffee-forward cities came back with new expectations, a desire for better coffee, and a curiosity about the craftsmanship behind it.

Local cafés responded to this shift by elevating their offerings. Oriole Coffee Roasters, which began its journey in 2008, was one of the first to capture this growing appreciation for specialty coffee. Their dedication to sourcing top-notch beans, training talented baristas, and celebrating the art of coffee raised the bar entirely. For many Singaporeans, Oriole was the place where they first discovered just how amazing a well-crafted cup of coffee could be.

This new approach also influenced the way cafés were designed. Unlike the functional, high-turnover setups of chain coffee shops, specialty cafés embraced a different philosophy. Interiors became more intentional, reflecting the care that went into every cup. Minimalist aesthetics, raw industrial finishes, and warm wooden elements created a sense of space that encouraged customers to linger. Open-concept bars, like the one at Chye Seng Huat Hardware, removed the traditional barriers between barista and customer, inviting people to witness the brewing process up close. It was an experience that extended beyond taste: watching a pour-over being prepared, listening to the gentle hiss of steamed milk, and inhaling the aroma of freshly ground beans became part of the ritual.

While some welcomed this change, others viewed it with skepticism. For many, coffee was meant to be simple: strong, sweet, and familiar. The careful brewing methods, lighter roasts, and higher price tags of specialty coffee felt excessive. It seemed like a completely separate world, catering to a niche group instead of the average coffee drinker.

Cafés and roasters had to find a way to make this shift more approachable. The challenge was not about proving which type of coffee was better, but about showing that there was room for both. Some cafés began offering side-by-side options, allowing customers to choose between a kopi-style brew or a delicately balanced single-origin pour-over. Others introduced educational experiences, from simple conversations at the counter to structured tasting sessions that encouraged people to explore coffee in a way they hadn't before.

It was in the midst of this changing landscape that Dutch Colony Coffee Co. made its entrance. In 2013, Dutch Colony took a bold step by opening at Pasarbella's Farmers Market, a lively artisanal food space inspired by the busy markets of Melbourne and London. Pasarbella provided the perfect backdrop for what we were trying to achieve at Dutch Colony Coffee Co. Unlike traditional cafés in shopping malls or busy streets, Pasarbella had a different rhythm. People came to browse, to discover, to slow down. They weren't rushing in for a quick caffeine fix; they were open to exploring what was on offer. In this setting, Dutch Colony stood out. Customers watched as baristas carefully brewed each cup, measuring, pouring, and extracting with precision. They saw beans being weighed and ground fresh for every order. The process was part of the experience.

The response was immediate: customers who had never given much thought to the origins of their coffee started asking questions and slowly began to understand why specialty coffee is about more than just caffeine.

This moment marked a turning point for both Dutch Colony and specialty coffee in Singapore. The café's success demonstrated that there was room for both kopi and specialty coffee chains, showing that Singaporeans were ready to explore a coffee experience that went beyond habit and convenience, one that valued craft, quality, and the story behind every bean.

A New Community Hub

As specialty coffee became a larger part of Singapore's café scene, the experience around it deepened and extended to inviting people to be part of the process. Cafés evolved into spaces where conversations went beyond the usual chatter about daily life, and baristas became storytellers, guiding customers into a world they might never have thought to explore.

Cupping sessions played a big role in this evolution. Instead of simply drinking coffee, people were encouraged to taste it in a structured way. The process was immersive. Participants inhaled the fragrance of dry grounds, watched as hot water brought the coffee to life, and broke the crust of foam on the surface, releasing waves of aroma. Then came the tasting, with loud slurps that helped coat the entire palate and allowed even the subtlest notes to stand out.

Workshops and hands-on brewing classes added another layer to this learning. People who had never considered making coffee at home beyond instant packets or a basic coffee machine were now investing in hand grinders, pour-over setups, and scales. They were learning how to control variables like water temperature, brew time, and grind size, realizing that each adjustment changed the final cup.

With more people becoming interested in coffee beyond their daily cup, the need for structured education grew. In the mid-2000s, coffee academies in Singapore were few and far between. Those who wanted to deepen their knowledge had limited options, with only a handful of institutions providing training. Places like Boncafe, Cuppachoice, and Highlander Coffee were among the earliest to offer workshops and barista training, giving enthusiasts a way to sharpen their skills. The focus was largely practical, teaching how to steam milk, pull a balanced espresso shot, and execute latte art. At the time, specialty coffee was still in its early days in Singapore, so these courses catered more to baristas looking to work in cafés rather than the everyday coffee drinker.

Fast forward to today, and the landscape is unrecognizable compared to those early days. Specialty coffee education has evolved into something much bigger, with institutions like Bettr

Barista leading the way. Unlike the early training centers that primarily focused on skills for café work, Bettr Barista introduced a more structured, holistic approach to coffee education. They developed rigorous programs that covered everything from sensory training to sustainable sourcing. Their certification programs provided baristas with professional credentials, while their workshops invited everyday drinkers to explore coffee in ways they hadn't before.

Beyond technical training, Bettr Barista also brought a strong social mission into the picture. Their initiatives went beyond café training, focusing on empowering individuals from marginalized communities, providing them with skills that could lead to long-term careers in the coffee industry. This approach raised the standards of coffee knowledge in Singapore and made education in the field more accessible to a wider audience.

Soon, new academies emerged, each bringing a unique approach to making knowledge about coffee more accessible. Among them, Katalyst Coffee Academy stood out for its commitment to Inclusivity. Unlike traditional training centers that focused solely on aspiring baristas or café owners, Katalyst expanded its reach to students from the Institute of Technical Education (ITE), youth-at-risk, and individuals with Autism Spectrum Disorder (ASD). Through carefully designed programs, they created opportunities for students who might otherwise struggle to find a foothold in the workforce. Coffee, in this case, became a key tool for empowerment.

The initiative marked a significant shift in perspective. Coffee education was evolving into a tool for both personal and professional growth. In Singapore, more young people were starting to view coffee not as just a side job, but as a serious craft and a viable career path. Historically, working in coffee was often seen as a temporary gig, something to do before moving on to a more stable profession. But with the introduction of accessible and formalized training programs and clear pathways into the industry, this perception was beginning to change.

This shift was further reinforced by government initiatives like SkillsFuture, which introduced the WSQ (Workplace Skills Qualifications) programs. With dedicated courses in barista skills, brewing techniques, and coffee appreciation, these programs legitimized coffee training as a professional discipline. The government's investment in coffee education was a sign that the industry was being taken seriously. What was once considered a niche interest was now seen as a valuable skill set, contributing to Singapore's growing reputation as a hub for specialty coffee. Aspiring baristas and café owners now had clearer pathways into the industry, but the hunger for knowledge extended beyond those looking to build a career in coffee.

The growing curiosity gave rise to a new wave of public cupping sessions, where roasters opened their doors to anyone eager to taste, learn, and discuss coffee in a communal setting. Unlike traditional café experiences, where coffee is consumed with little thought about its origins, cupping sessions turned coffee into an interactive experience. These sessions became opportunities to learn firsthand how coffee from different regions carries distinct characteristics, shaped by everything from altitude to processing methods. Roasters like Common Man Coffee Roasters, Toby's Estate, and The

Coffee Academics took the lead in making these sessions widely available. They turned an industry practice into a social and educational experience, welcoming curious newcomers and seasoned professionals alike. Through these gatherings, coffee appreciation grew beyond café counters and into a shared cultural experience.

More than anything, these cupping events created a sense of openness and transparency in the specialty coffee community. They allowed roasters to share insights into their sourcing practices, discuss roasting techniques, and highlight the work of coffee farmers in a way that made every cup feel more meaningful.

With every workshop, cupping session, and café visit, the appreciation for coffee continues to grow. More people are becoming curious about where their coffee comes from, how it is processed, and what makes each cup taste different. The desire to understand the craft has led to deeper conversations between customers and baristas, creating a more engaged and informed coffee culture.

Coffee shops have also evolved. Today's coffee scenes are immersive, where the ambiance of a café is as important as the quality of the brew. Spaces like these are where people come together to experience and savor coffee, learn about its intricacies, and connect with others who share similar passions.

This evolution shows no signs of slowing down. For me, one of the most rewarding moments in this evolution of specialty coffee has always been that first sip, the one that changes everything. I have seen it happen countless times. A customer, someone who has spent years drinking coffee the same way, takes a sip of something brewed differently: a pour-over, a siphon, or a single-origin that carries flavors they never expected. There's a pause. A flicker of surprise. And then, a realization that coffee can be something entirely new. I have watched this moment unfold across counters, at cupping sessions, and even in casual conversations over a shared pot of coffee. No matter how many times I witness it, the feeling never fades.

It's these moments that remind me why coffee continues to evolve, why the industry pushes forward, and why those of us in it stay curious. Coffee is not static. It moves with time, with culture, and with the people who drink it. It has the power to surprise, to challenge expectations, and to open doors to a deeper appreciation of flavor, craftsmanship, and history. Watching someone experience that shift in perspective, to see them go from drinking coffee as a habit to savoring it as an experience, is what makes this industry so alive.

More than anything, the beauty of coffee lies in its ability to bring people together. I have met people from every walk of life through coffee: farmers who pour their hearts into their crops, baristas who strive for perfection in every cup, and customers who are eager to learn, to taste, to explore. Coffee sparks conversations, builds friendships, and creates a sense of community that extends far beyond a single café or a single cup.

One of the best examples of this camaraderie in action was the regular gatherings held at Oriole Café and the Cuppachoice Academy in Chinatown. Almost every weekend, the doors would open to an impromptu jam session behind the bar. Some would bring their latest roasts, eager to get feedback. Others would introduce a new brewing method they had been experimenting with. It was unstructured, informal, and yet deeply enriching.

The best part was that it never felt like a competition. There was no gatekeeping, no ego. Everyone was there to learn, to share, and to grow together. Someone would pull a shot on the espresso machine while another person adjusted the grind, testing out how small tweaks could affect the final cup. A fresh batch of beans would be roasted on-site, filling the space with the familiar, comforting aroma of caramelizing coffee oils. The excitement of discovery made each session feel new, even if we had gathered at the same spot week after week.

It was in these moments that I met some of the people who would go on to shape my journey in coffee: John Ting, Terence Tan, Keith Low, Danny Hor, Fadhly, and Noribsham. Each of them brought their own approach, their own philosophy, and their own curiosity to the table. What started as casual meetups soon became friendships built on a shared passion. Customers who had initially come in just for a cup of coffee found themselves drawn into the conversations, eventually becoming regulars. Some of them, like Andrew and James Tan, stayed in my life long after those early days. Nearly two decades later, we still keep in touch, bound by memories of those afternoons spent experimenting, debating, and laughing over countless cups of coffee.

An especially inspiring story from those gatherings was that of Lee Hee Wei. He was an engineer by trade, someone whose career had been built on accuracy, structure, and problem-solving. But coffee had a way of pulling people in, and for Hee

Wei, what started as curiosity quickly turned into something much bigger. Between 2010 and 2011, he attended a series of barista workshops, eager to learn the craft.

I remember watching him during those sessions, the way he focused on every movement, every extraction, every pour. He approached coffee the way an engineer would, breaking it down into variables, testing different factors, and searching for that perfect balance. And yet, despite all the technical precision, something deeper was at play. For him, coffee was turning into a calling.

Not long after, Hee Wei took a leap that many would have hesitated to make. He left engineering behind to start his own coffee journey. At first, he operated a small coffee cart, serving carefully brewed cups to customers who, like him, were beginning to appreciate coffee in a new way. Slowly, his venture grew. The coffee cart turned into a full-fledged café. And then, in what felt like a full-circle moment, he stepped onto the competition stage. Hee Wei became one of Singapore's Barista Champions in the Singapore National Barista Championship (SNBC), cementing his place in the very community that had once inspired him to make that first jump.

His story shows how coffee can truly change lives. It's easy to think of coffee as just a drink, something we pick up on the way to work or sip during meetings. But for some, it changes the course of their lives. It gives them purpose, a craft to master, a path they never expected to walk.

Looking back at those early days, I see them for what they truly were: the foundation of a movement where people could take risks, reinvent themselves, and push the boundaries of what coffee could be. There was an unspoken understanding that we were all part of something new, something bigger than ourselves. We weren't just making coffee. We were shaping the future of it in Singapore, one conversation, one experiment, and one cup at a time.

CHAPTER 5

The Café Renaissance

During this time of slowly brewing a new coffee future in the city-state, an exciting chapter unfolded following the 2010 Singapore National Barista Championship. That year, John Ting had just been crowned the National Champion, Keith Loh, the founder of Oriole Coffee Roasters, had secured second place, and I had secured third place. The energy from the competition was still fresh, and as the evening progressed, Oriole hosted Singapore's first-ever Latte Art Throwdown, an event that felt almost surreal at the time.

Walking through the doors of Oriole Coffee Roasters at Republic Plaza for the first time, I felt something shift. There was an unmistakable electricity in the space, something that reminded me of the way history books describe the Renaissance, an era when creativity, knowledge, and craftsmanship converged to reshape the world.

Baristas moved behind the counter with the kind of confidence I had only seen in competition settings. The crowd leaned in, some holding their breath as patterns emerged in the cups. Rosettas, tulips, and swans formed effortlessly with each pour. There was no hesitation or second-guessing, only fluid motion and the kind of precision that turned coffee-making into a performance. The café itself was a world apart from anything I had seen in Singapore. A towering retail wall stretched from floor to ceiling, packed with books, brewing gadgets, and barista tools that, until then, had felt like distant luxuries. I had spent years reading about these things in magazines and online forums, wishing I could get my hands on them. And now, they were right in front of me, as if the world of specialty coffee had suddenly materialized in this very space.

Behind the counter, a La Marzocco espresso machine gleamed under the café's warm lighting. The polished steel of the Mazzer grinders beside it caught the golden glow of the room, while the rich aroma of freshly brewed espresso lingered throughout. I had always associated setups like this with the coffee capitals of Melbourne and San Francisco. But standing there, taking in the scene around me, I realized this wasn't something distant anymore. It was happening here, in Singapore, unfolding right in front of me.

Keith stood behind the counter with his arms crossed, quietly taking in the crowd with a satisfied look. He caught my eye and nodded toward John, who was completely in his element, effortlessly pulling espresso shots."You're looking at the future," Keith said. I smiled, nodding in agreement, because I could see it too. The café, once just a functional spot for quick transactions, was evolving into a stage for craftsmanship and a hub where ideas could flourish. Singapore was on the brink of its own café renaissance.

The Places That Shaped the Scene

This café renaissance marked a shift in mindset nurtured by those who were willing to take risks, to push beyond what was familiar, and to introduce something new to a city where coffee had long been about routine and familiarity. While I've briefly mentioned the contributions of certain cafés and roasters previously, I want to slow down and dive deeper into the spaces that shaped this movement. These were the places where ideas were exchanged, where boundaries were pushed, and where a new culture took root.

A key moment in this shift was the arrival of Toby's Estate. I've touched on my time there before, but what Toby's did for Singapore's coffee scene was something that deserves a deeper look. Sitting along the Singapore River, the café and roastery brought with it an approach to coffee that was new for many locals. The emphasis was on sourcing beans directly from farmers, roasting them in a way that highlighted their natural flavors, and brewing with techniques that focused on precision and clarity. Customers were engaged in the process, exploring different beans, brewing methods, and tasting notes.

At the same time, homegrown cafés like Nylon Coffee Roasters began making their mark. Tucked within Everton Park, far from the busy café districts, it didn't rely on foot traffic or flashy branding to build its reputation. Instead, it drew people in through one thing: quality. Nylon was one of the first cafés to strip things down to the essentials, removing the distractions of elaborate menus and large-scale operations. Their focus was purely on the coffee.

The founders, Dennis Tang and Jia Min Lee,built something special that reflected their commitment to ethical sourcing and the relationships they had formed with farmers around the world. They traveled to coffee farms with a direct trade approach, ensuring farmers were fairly paid and gaining a deep understanding of the coffee's journey from origin to cup.

Amidst that time, another café was making waves in a very different way: Common Man Coffee Roasters (CMCR). It entered the scene in 2013 with a vision that wanted to change the way people thought about the profession of coffee itself. Unlike Nylon, which focused on the purity of the coffee experience, CMCR took a more holistic approach, blending café culture with coffee education.

Stepping into CMCR felt different from walking into a traditional café. The space was designed as a place where baristas weren't only serving coffee but mastering a craft. Their Barista Academy became one of the most respected training grounds for coffee professionals, offering courses that covered everything from fundamental brewing techniques to advanced latte art. It also attracted enthusiastic home brewers, café owners, and curious coffee drinkers. CMCR's impact extended beyond training. Their commitment to ethical sourcing helped raise awareness of sustainability in coffee. That consciousness rippled through the industry, influencing the way other cafés approached sourcing and transparency.

CMCR's influence is also evident in its sister café, 40 Hands. When it opened in October 2010, Tiong Bahru was still a quiet residential district, known more for its heritage charm than for café culture. That started to change the moment 40 Hands set up shop. Founded by Harry Grover in collaboration with the Spa Esprit Group, the café was one of the first to introduce Third Wave coffee to Singapore. It blended a modern café experience with a nostalgic nod to local kopitiam culture, showing that specialty coffee could happily coexist with tradition. 40 Hands also adopted sustainability by prioritizing fair trade and direct trade beans, highlighting the collective effort behind every cup. In fact, the name 40 Hands says it all, honoring the 40 pairs of hands it takes, from farmers to roasters to baristas, to bring coffee from the farm to your cup.

Beyond its espresso-based drinks, the café became a gathering place, serving Australian-style brunches and creating a sense of community that hadn't been seen before in the neighborhood. It was a café that showed what was possible when quality coffee, thoughtful sourcing, and a welcoming space came together. For almost 12 years, 40 Hands was a key part of Singapore's specialty coffee scene. When it shut down its Tiong Bahru and East Coast locations in September 2022, it truly felt like the end of an era.

While cafés like 40 Hands reshaped how people experienced coffee in neighborhood settings, Jewel Coffee was gaining attention in the heart of Singapore's business district.Founded by Adrian Khong in 2011, Jewel Coffee brought specialty coffee to the fast-paced world of Shenton Way, where coffee had long been treated as a quick necessity rather than something to savor.

Unlike most cafés in the area, which focused on convenience and consistency, Jewel Coffee introduced something different: high-quality, single-origin coffees that rotated frequently. Customers who were used to ordering their usual latte or long black suddenly had options from Tanzania, Kenya, Brazil, and Guatemala, each with distinct flavor profiles. The café's menu encouraged people to explore coffee beyond the standard house blends that were common elsewhere. This rotation of beans allowed customers to experience how origin, processing, and roasting influenced flavor.

Jewel Coffee also embraced alternative brewing methods at a time when they were rarely seen outside of competitions or high-end specialty cafés. Chemex, V60, and siphon brews were available alongside espresso drinks, giving customers the chance to taste coffee through different lenses. Over time, what started as a single specialty café in the financial district expanded across Singapore, growing into one of the island's largest homegrown specialty coffee chains.

Soon, cafés began finding new ways to set themselves apart. The focus was on creating experiences that extended beyond the cup. This shift led to cafés that told stories, deeply rooted in heritage, culture, and identity. Kafe Utu was a prime example of this. More than a café, it was an expression of African culture in the heart of Singapore. From the moment you stepped inside, the space felt like an invitation to explore a world not often represented in the local coffee scene. The walls were adorned with African art, the furniture was rich with warm textures, and the atmosphere carried an energy that made it feel distinct. The coffee menu paid homage to Africa's role as the birthplace of coffee, featuring beans from Ethiopia, Kenya, and Tanzania, each roasted to highlight the unique flavors of their origins. Alongside the coffee, the café served dishes inspired by African cuisine, blending the flavors of the continent with a specialty coffee experience.

Tanamera Coffee carried a similar philosophy but with a focus on Indonesia. When it expanded to Singapore, it introduced a perspective that was often missing from the specialty coffee scene. While most cafés were sourcing their beans from Africa or Latin America, Tanamera shone a light on the diverse coffee-growing regions of Indonesia. It gave Singaporeans a chance to experience the depth of Indonesian coffee, from the chocolatey richness of Sumatra to the bright, fruity notes of Bali. It went on to integrate coffee with traditional Indonesian cuisine, creating a space where people could appreciate the country's coffee culture in its full form. This connection between coffee and food was central to the experience, proving that specialty coffee could thrive within the framework of existing culinary traditions.

Other cafés have taken inspiration from design, music, and multi-sensory experiences. The Glasshouse, with its sun-drenched space and lush greenery, felt more like a retreat than a café. The tall windows framed the soft, natural light that poured in, casting shadows over wooden counters where coffee was brewed with precision. It was the kind of place where you could sit for hours, letting time slow down with every sip.

Apartment Coffee took a different approach, one that was quiet, intentional, and stripped of anything unnecessary. Located at Lavender Street before moving to Selegie Road, it was a space that felt more like a carefully designed home than a typical café. The clean white walls, soft natural light, and Scandinavian-style furniture created a sense of calm, making every visit feel unhurried. There were no elaborate food menus or branded merchandise, no distractions pulling attention away from what mattered most: the coffee.

The café was founded by Yeo Qing He, a former Singapore Brewers Cup Champion who had also placed sixth in the World Brewers Cup in Brazil. His approach to coffee was reflected in every detail of the space. The minimalism was focused on creating an environment where the connection between the barista and the customer felt personal.

Beyond the well-known names, smaller cafés emerged in unexpected places, turning quiet neighborhoods into destinations. Percolate in Bedok showed that a great cup of coffee didn't have to be confined to the central business district. Its presence brought a new energy to the area, offering carefully brewed coffee to a community that had once been overlooked by the specialty scene. Glyph Supply Co. took a different approach, combining sleek, futuristic design with a rotating selection of coffees, drawing in a younger crowd eager to explore different flavors and brewing styles.

Some cafés merged coffee with food and cultural influences, creating experiences that extended beyond the drink. Baristart Coffee introduced a uniquely Japanese touch, incorporating Hokkaido milk into its offerings, creating a bridge between specialty coffee and Japan's deep appreciation for quality dairy.

Others, like Five Oars Coffee Roasters, channeled Melbourne's contemporary café culture with its warehouse-style interiors and experimental approach to brewing. The café first made its mark in Tanjong Pagar before eventually moving to East Coast Road. In its earlier days, the café had an industrial, almost raw aesthetic with concrete floors, exposed pipes, and an open space that gave it an experimental edge. When it relocated, the atmosphere took on a warmer, more rustic feel.

Earthy tones replaced the stark industrial look, and tropical plants softened the space, creating a setting that felt both refreshing and familiar. Beyond the coffee, its menu evolved into something that balanced innovation with comfort. Brunch favorites like Valrhona chocolate pancakes and housemade rosti with poached eggs became just as much of a draw as the coffee itself. It was this ability to bring together high-quality brews with thoughtful, well-crafted dishes that cemented its reputation in Singapore's specialty coffee scene.

Walking into Five Oars today, I can still see hints of its beginnings, the boldness, the experimentation, the influence of Melbourne's café culture. There's also a sense of how it has grown, adapting to the tastes and rhythms of the local crowd while staying true to its roots. It's places like this that continue to shape Singapore's café renaissance evolving with each new step while never losing sight of what made them stand out in the first place.

The Art of Space

As the café renaissance gathered pace, design also became a defining part of the café experience. Some cafés blended coffee culture with visual arts, transforming their spaces into mini-galleries where the walls told stories alongside the brews being served. Artistry Café was one of these places. Situated along Jalan Pinang, it combined specialty coffee with a lively arts scene, hosting exhibitions, poetry readings, and live performances. It wasn't uncommon here to sip on a perfectly crafted latte while watching an artist set up an installation or hearing a poet recite their latest work.

Telok Ayer Arts Club took this concept even further, merging coffee, food, cocktails, and contemporary art under one roof. It was a place where boundaries blurred, where a café could double as an art studio, and a cup of coffee could be the start of a conversation about design, culture, or music.

These cafés built something special, spaces that felt alive with creativity and purpose. But the café scene in Singapore has always been dynamic, shifting with time. Artistry Café and Telok Ayer Arts Club eventually closed their doors, a reminder that even the most beloved spaces must evolve or risk fading away. Their legacy, however, remains. They proved that a café could be a cultural hub, a stage for artists, and a meeting point for ideas waiting to take shape.

Global brands have also played a role in shaping how café spaces are experienced. These brands bring their own philosophies, redefining how design and coffee interact. Some focus on bold, architectural statements, while others create spaces that encourage stillness and mindfulness.

% Arabica is one such brand. Known for its signature clean style, every % Arabica café is a showcase of precision and simplicity. Their spaces are carefully curated, with natural materials, smooth surfaces, and an open-concept design that allows customers to watch the baristas work with unwavering focus. In Singapore, their cafés reflect the same careful attention to detail, effortlessly blending into their surroundings while still standing out. Stepping into a % Arabica café feels like entering a world of perfect order, where every action behind the bar is deliberate and almost feels like a beautifully choreographed performance.

Blue Bottle Coffee, on the other hand, leans into a different kind of simplicity. Inspired by Japanese and Scandinavian design principles, their cafés have a warmth that draws people in. Wooden tones, soft lighting, and uncluttered interiors create a space that encourages people to slow down. In Japan and Korea, Blue Bottle's cafés take this philosophy even further, creating an environment that feels more like a sanctuary than a coffee shop.

Recently, the intersection of fashion, retail, and coffee has become another growing trend. The presence of specialty coffee within fashion boutiques and concept stores signaled that coffee had become part of a larger lifestyle. Brands like Coach, Editor's Market, and Ralph Lauren introduced in-store cafés, allowing customers to sip on carefully brewed coffee while browsing collections. These spaces encouraged shoppers to linger and experience the store in a different way. A well-pulled espresso could turn a routine shopping trip into something more personal and memorable. On a local level, The Alchemist adopted this trend, opening a café within Funan, a mall known for its curated mix of retail, tech, and creative spaces.

Interestingly, Singapore had seen an early version of this concept long before it became mainstream. In the late 1990s and early 2000s, Project Shop Blood Brothers, a pioneering local fashion label, introduced a café experience within its retail space. The combination of edgy fashion and a laid-back coffee culture appealed to customers, and over time, the café aspect took on a life of its own. That concept eventually evolved into PS.Cafe, which grew into a well-loved dining institution known for its stylish interiors, indulgent menu, and deeply rooted café culture.

From gallery-inspired cafés to retail hybrids, the way cafés are designed today is a reflection of something deeper. They are curated spaces that invite interaction, evoke emotion, and leave an impression. Whether it's through unique architecture, creative art, or cultural storytelling, Singapore's cafés are constantly evolving, playing a key role in the city's thriving social and creative scene.

Cafés as Catalysts for Craft

Looking back at this café renaissance, I realize that these cafés became catalysts for something much bigger: the craft of specialty coffee itself. These cafés created an environment where curiosity thrived, where conversations about coffee turned into friendships, and where a single sip could shift someone's entire perspective.

I have seen it happen firsthand. Many customers who once believed coffee was simply a morning routine found themselves completely absorbed by the world of specialty coffee. I remember Karen, who first walked into a coffee tasting out of curiosity, expecting nothing more than a casual experience. She sat quietly, observing, unsure of what to look for in the flavors. Then, she took a sip of a naturally processed Ethiopian coffee. I could see the moment of realization hit. Her eyes widened as she tried to make sense of what she was tasting. It wasn't just strong or bitter. It was bright and layered with flavors she never expected from coffee.

That single experience changed something in her. A few months later, she was showing up to every cupping session, notebook in hand, scribbling tasting notes and asking more questions than most baristas-in-training. Years later, she opened her own small coffee shop, and whenever our paths cross, she still reminds me how that one cup set everything in motion. Cafés have played this role over and over again, opening doors for people to discover a new side of coffee.

Another inspiring example that comes to mind is Fadhly's. When he first came into the scene, he was eager but unsure of where he fit in. He had a deep appreciation for coffee, but like many who start out, he wasn't certain if it was something he could turn into a career. That uncertainty didn't last long. He trained with focus, developing skills both as a barista and a roaster, constantly seeking to refine his craft. His hunger to learn set him apart, and over time, that dedication opened doors. Today, he serves as the Head of Specialty Desk at Bero Coffee, a respected name in Singapore's coffee industry. Watching his journey unfold has been a reminder of how passion, when met with the right environment and opportunities, can transform into something remarkable.

Jamal, another talented individual, had a path that was different but just as inspiring. From the start, he was drawn to the mechanics of espresso extraction. He wasn't satisfied with just pulling shots; he wanted to understand the science behind every variable, from grind size to water temperature, and how each one influenced the final cup. At the same time, he found himself captivated by the roasting process, awed by how different profiles could unlock entirely new dimensions in a coffee's flavor. His persistence and attention to detail eventually led him to a leadership role in QC and roasting for Olam, now Ofi, a major player in global coffee sourcing.

Then there's Mustakim. He started out as the Head Barista at Dutch Colony, honing his craft behind the bar, refining his skills in both brewing and customer service. But beyond the technical aspects, he had a vision to build something of his own. That vision took shape when he ventured out to start Meadow Brew in Ang Mo Kio. Today, Meadow Brew has become a neighborhood staple, a café where regulars stop by for a well-brewed cup and stay for the conversations.

Another barista who made his mark early on at Dutch Colony was Siraj. His technical skill and ability to push the boundaries of brewing stood out, and he proved his expertise when he won the ASEAN Barista Challenge. But competition wasn't the end of the road for him; it was the beginning of a new chapter. Today, he plays a key role in shaping the coffee program at Kwaasong, a bakery that is redefining the relationship between coffee and pastries. His work bridges two worlds, showing how a deep understanding of coffee can enhance everything it touches, even beyond the walls of a café.

Over the years, I've had the privilege of watching these journeys unfold as people step into the world of coffee with nothing but curiosity and walk away with a lifelong pursuit. Some started as customers, drawn in by the smell of fresh brews and the ritual of a morning cup. Others, like Karen and the engineer-turned-café owner Lee Hee Wei, whom I mentioned in the last chapter, went from casual drinkers to dedicated professionals, shaping the very scene they once admired from the sidelines. Their stories have always inspired me because of how they got there: through a strong passion, an openness to learning, and a deep sense of community.

Recently, as I was working on this book, I reached out to Hee Wei. I wanted to hear his thoughts now that he had built his own place in the café renaissance. "Did you ever imagine this is where coffee would take you?" I asked him.

He laughed, the same easygoing laugh I remembered from years ago. "Not in my wildest dreams. But that's the thing about coffee, it connects people, opens doors, and always pushes you to explore. The community we built back then is what gave me the courage to take that leap."

That conversation stayed with me. It reminded me that these journeys are about the people who come together, the friendships forged over shared experiences, and the way one simple moment, like a cup, a conversation, or a new discovery, can set off an entire chain of events.

These same journeys prepared me for something I hadn't anticipated: becoming a café co-owner in 2014 with Dutch Colony. The relationships I built over the years, the lessons I learned from mentors and peers, and the countless hours spent behind the counter and at cupping tables all led me to that moment. When I think about it now, it's funny how things unfolded. Much like Hee Wei, I never imagined myself taking this path.

People often ask me if I had always dreamed of owning a café, given how many years I spent working in them. My answer is always the same. “Nope. Because I've seen it all.” Running a café is tough. It's long hours, endless problem-solving, and constant adaptation. If you had asked me back then what I wanted to open, I would have probably told you about my dream of starting a laksa or Thai beef noodle shop when I reached retirement age.

But as life often does, it threw an opportunity my way that I couldn't ignore.

Despite my initial hesitation, something about the opportunity felt right. It wasn't the dream of being my own boss. It wasn't the idea of starting a business. It was the people. It felt like an extension of the relationships I had built over the years, a place where people could gather, learn, and grow in their appreciation for coffee. More than anything, it was about creating a space where passion could thrive.

As I move forward in this story, I'll be sharing more about my journey as a café owner, including the challenges, the lessons, and the moments that shaped my perspective. But for now, as I think about everything that has led me to this point, one thing is clear. The café renaissance in Singapore has been as much about the people as it is about the cafés themselves. It has been built by the baristas who push their craft further each day, by the café owners who create spaces that bring people together, and by the customers who come in for the experience of it all. In the end, coffee is what brings us to the table, but it is the relationships we build that make us stay.

BUHLER
DUTCH COLONY
DUTCH COLONY

SPONSORS
BUNN
ditting
knockhouse

INDOGA

ORGANIZED BY
BARISTA GUILD INDONESIA
ICE 2017 INDONESIA
COFFEE
5 - 8 APRIL 2017
2017 INDONESIA BARISTA CHAMPIONSHIP
BrookFarm

APPRECIATING KALDI
& THE BERRIES

GOLDEN

Singapore
National Barista

ICE2017 INDONESIA COFFEE EVENTS
5 - 8 APRIL 2017
LATTE ART

ASEAN Barista Championship 2013

EXIT

EXIT
TOBY'S ESTATE

coffee t&i

TOBY'S ESTATE
HAPPENINGS
EVENTS
FLAT WHITE WEDNESDAY!

TOBY'S

National Barista
Championship
21 - 23 March 2011

21 - 23 March 2011

DUTCH COLONY

CHAPTER 6

Masters Behind the Counter

If the café renaissance in Singapore were a canvas, the baristas would be the ones holding the brushes, bringing it to life with every pour, every swirl of milk, and every carefully measured shot of espresso. Much like the painters of the Renaissance who shaped their era with bold strokes and delicate details, these baristas have crafted a movement of their own, one that goes beyond the mechanics of making coffee and into something closer to an art form.

I think back to my own days behind the counter. If there was one moment in the day that truly captured the energy of a café, it was the morning rush. The world outside was still waking up, but behind the bar, the scent of freshly ground coffee lingered, accompanied by the steady tamping of grounds and the hiss of steaming milk rising into the morning. The machines were never silent, the grinders buzzed like restless engines, and the steady clink of portafilters being locked in and out of the espresso machine created a pattern that was impossible to ignore.

There was a kind of choreography to it all, with movements honed over time and sharpened by muscle memory. Hands reaching for the knock box, wrists flicking to distribute coffee grounds evenly, a quick glance at the shot timer before the next cup was queued. The pace never slowed. Orders piled up, shouted over the counter in a seamless exchange, and yet, even in the chaos, there was a kind of flow. A barista who had mastered the morning shift knew how to keep that rhythm alive, moving from one task to the next without hesitation.

I remember the weight of the milk pitchers in my hands, the way the steam wand roared to life, stretching and swirling the milk until it was the right consistency—smooth, glossy, warm enough to blend without overpowering the espresso. The trick was in the timing, in knowing when to stop before it turned too hot, before the texture lost its silkiness. The first few times I tried, I fumbled, overshot the temperature, or ended up with milk too thin to hold any shape. But with time, it became second nature. I could hear when the milk was ready just by the change in pitch, the subtle shift in sound from a sharp hiss to something softer, almost like a whisper.

There was never a moment to pause, but in some strange way, that was what made it exhilarating. The orders kept coming: long blacks, flat whites, cappuccinos with extra foam, the occasional oat milk request that required a quick swap of the pitcher.

Morning shifts were always about holding the energy of the café together. A barista who worked the morning rush learned to read people without needing to ask: the hurried professionals who needed their coffee fast, the ones who paused just long enough for small talk before rushing off, the silent nod exchanged with a regular who came in at the same time every single day.

It was in these moments, in the heat of the rush, that I learned what it meant to stand behind the counter. To move with instinct. To balance speed with precision. To work in sync with the team, passing cups down the line without needing to speak. You simply became part of the rhythm, hands moving, cups stacking, orders flowing, the café coming alive in the hands of those who worked it.

And nowhere was this rhythm more evident than during my time working in Singapore's lively CBD at Starbucks. Helming the bar in a café surrounded by towering office buildings, I quickly saw how coffee fueled the city. People streamed in like clockwork, their routines as precise as the machines we worked behind. The regulars didn't even need to order; by the time they reached the counter, their drinks were already in the making.

"Hey Lionel, your usual?" I'd call out before he could even step forward.

Lionel worked at DBS, just behind the alley of Robinson Road. He barely looked up from his phone as he nodded, still checking his emails. By the time he tapped his card on the reader, his Americano was ready, the lid snapped on, sleeve wrapped neatly around the cup. He'd take it without breaking stride, already walking toward the exit before I could say, "Have a good one!"

Then there was Mrs. Chan, who had been coming in every weekday for as long as I could remember. She was in her late fifties, always dressed in sharp pencil skirts and crisp blouses, her heels clicking against the tiles as she approached the counter. She never had to say a word. Her order, a latte, extra hot, with an extra shot of espresso, was already in motion the second she stepped through the door.

Unlike Lionel, she lingered. While waiting, she'd glance at the baristas, her eyes sharp, scanning our movements. "Too much milk today, ah?" she'd say with the faintest smile, watching me work the steam wand. I had learned early on that with Mrs. Chan, consistency mattered.

One morning, mid-rush, I caught her watching from her usual spot by the pick-up counter, arms folded. When I passed her the cup, she held it for a moment, testing the weight. Then, as if awarding a final grade, she nodded. "Better," she murmured before walking off.

And then there was Faizal, a civil engineer who worked on site most days but always stopped by before heading into the office. He was the one customer I associated most with laughter. His voice carried above the noise of the crowd, effortlessly filling the space.

"Oi, Suhaimi!" he'd call out before even reaching the counter. "I hope you made it strong today. I've got a meeting so dry, even my coffee needs coffee."

His grande caramel macchiato, less sweet, was already being prepared as he stood there chatting, occasionally throwing a joke at the next customer in line. He had a way of making people smile, even those who had just stepped out of the MRT, still half-asleep. He'd take his drink, raise it in a little toast to us, and walk out the door, leaving behind a pocket of warmth in the otherwise fast-moving crowd.

It was in these fleeting, everyday moments that I could clearly see that, for many, coffee was their fuel, their comfort, and the one predictable thing in a day full of moving targets. And yet, even in all its familiarity, the rush was never the same twice.

This daily ritual reminded me of the kopi trade in traditional kopitiams, where the kopi uncles would see a familiar face and, without a word, start brewing their usual. When I was younger, tagging along with my Ayah or Atuk to the neighborhood kopitiam, I used to marvel at how these uncles seemed to know everyone. They never needed a written order. A glance, a nod, a wave of the hand—everything was understood. The regulars had their own way of asking for their drinks, sometimes with a simple lift of their fingers. Two fingers meant kopi C, three meant kopi-O kosong.

After all these years, even in these busy cafes, the rhythm, that unspoken connection between customer and server, remained the same. Some ordered with full sentences, others with grunts. Some wanted their coffee extra hot, others with a dash of vanilla, or with a lid but no sleeve to feel the warmth in their hands. It was in these small, personal details that trust was formed.

That was my first real lesson in speed, consistency, and connection. You had to anticipate, remember, and execute, all in the span of seconds. The right grind size, the perfect milk texture, the correct order, every single time. A single mistake, too much foam, a weak shot, the wrong syrup, meant breaking that trust, even if it was just for a day. But even in the blur of orders and the hiss of steaming milk, I knew this wasn't my final stop. By 2009, my coffee journey took a sharp turn.

I had stepped away from the corporate coffee world and into something that felt equally exciting and terrifying: co-owning a café, academy, retail space, and roastery in Temple Street, Chinatown. Cuppachoice Pte Ltd was a side venture with my boss, separate from the main company, Cuppachoice International Pte Ltd, where I was still a salaried employee handling sales and training. The arrangement was complicated. I had one foot in a stable job and another in a risky business, trying to balance both without slipping.

At the café, I was the only one who had real F&B experience, which meant I had to juggle multiple roles as trainer, manager, roaster, and barista, all while keeping up with my corporate responsibilities. Some days, I was on the floor, pulling shots and managing the morning rush. Other days, I was in the roasting room, fine-tuning profiles and packaging wholesale orders. At night, I was at my desk, handling invoices, writing training modules, and preparing sales reports. It was everything I had wanted to do with coffee, to teach, serve, and sell, but it also meant stepping into the unknown.

I once wrote in my blog:

"Today, 11 years ago, I was a co-owner of a small-time café, academy, and roastery all in one. I was 29 years old in this photo, and it was complicated.

"I joined this traditional coffee family business in 2007, fresh after an eight-year stint with Starbucks. I was a salaried employee, cutting my teeth in sales and training for this coffee company—roasting and selling commercial-grade Arabica coffees.

"Two years later, in 2009, we opened another entity, separated from the traditional business, and conceptualized this 'roaster in a box' concept, opening one unit away from the famous Sia Huat. I was made Director with a 30% shareholding. Business

was brisk, the academy was doing well, and we were selling specialty-graded single origins in 200g bags, always overselling each week's roasted batches."

That small space on Temple Street was a classroom, a workshop, and a testing ground for ideas that weren't common in Singapore at the time. Baristas came in as students, some knowing only the basics, others eager to perfect their craft. We trained them in extraction techniques, milk texturing, sensory evaluation, and everything that went into making a great cup. Some took to it like they were born for it, others struggled, but every one of them learned that behind every effortless pour, there were hours of practice.

This place became a breeding ground for talent. Many of the baristas who trained here went on to shape the industry, some as café owners, others as head baristas, and a few even rising to become competition champions. There was a kind of pride in watching them step onto bigger stages, knowing that their journeys had passed through these very doors.

The roastery itself became something more than we had planned. We started toll-roasting for baristas competing on stage. These were people who cared about their coffee down to the smallest variable, how the beans were sourced, how they were processed, what altitude they were grown at, and how they were roasted to bring out the best in them.

The grind was relentless. There was hardly a day to rest, a continuous cycle of sales, training, brewing, and roasting that blurred the lines between work and life. There were days when I barely saw my family. My wife would bring our daughter to the café so I could steal a few minutes with her between orders. I would kneel beside her, brushing coffee dust off my apron before scooping her into my arms, inhaling the faint trace of baby powder on her skin. She would tug at my collar, giggling, completely unaware of how exhausted I was. Those moments were short, sometimes no longer than the time it took for a fresh batch of espresso to finish pouring, but they meant everything. Before I could settle into them, I was back at the machines, wiping down the steam wand, calling out another order, and watching the café come back to life.

I told myself that this was part of the process, that this was what it took to make something work. What I didn't realize then was that it was also setting the foundation for an even bigger challenge ahead. After two years, I took on a new role as Café Manager and Roaster at Toby's Estate, a position that came with its own unique challenges. As I had mentioned in the previous chapters, Toby's Estate was renowned for its high standards and was one of Australia's top coffee brands. There was an unspoken understanding that every barista working that bar had to be at the top of their game. If you were on shift, you had to be prepared to deliver, no matter how chaotic the rush was.

I found myself working alongside industry veterans like Terence Tan, Nizam Mosta, and Andy Rohmat, baristas whose names were already cemented in the Singapore coffee scene. Some of them had been competitors in national championships, others had years of experience in specialty coffee. I had brewed alongside some of them before, but this time, we weren't in a competition setting. We were in a café that never slowed down, and every single order was a test of skill and focus.

The café was packed from the moment we unlocked the doors, with a constant line of customers who knew exactly what they wanted. There was no room for hesitation. The first shot of espresso had to be as perfect as the hundredth, the milk had to be aerated at the right temperature, the latte art had to be crisp, not a single pour sloppy or rushed.

Industry leaders and coffee professionals often stopped by, not for casual conversations, but to see if the coffee held up to the name. Some would take a sip, pause for a moment, and nod slightly before walking off. Others would glance at the bar, their eyes scanning the workflow, watching how efficiently orders were handled, how steady our hands were, how seamlessly we moved from one drink to the next. There was no need for feedback. If you were trusted to be behind the bar at Toby's, it meant you had already proven yourself. Every movement had to be deliberate, and every cup had to count.

Barista Culture in Singapore: The Rise of the Coffee Craftsman

My own journey showed me that the role of a barista has evolved far beyond being the person taking orders and making drinks. In Singapore's specialty coffee scene, baristas have become craftsmen, storytellers, and ambassadors of the coffee experience.

The rise of third-wave coffee changed everything. Cafés became spaces where coffee was studied, experimented with, and appreciated in ways that were once reserved for fine wines and gourmet cuisine. To meet this demand, specialty cafés began investing heavily in training. Baristas were no longer learning on the job through trial and error. They were sent for structured workshops, attended cupping sessions, and participated in brewing and sensory skill programs. Some even had the opportunity to travel overseas, visiting coffee farms, meeting producers, and understanding coffee from its very roots. These experiences shaped the way they worked behind the bar. A barista who had stood in the middle of a farm in Colombia or Ethiopia, watching the cherries being harvested, would never look at a bag of beans the same way again.

Mentorship also became a defining part of the industry. Experienced baristas took younger ones under their wing, guiding them through the complexities of extraction, milk texturing, and the delicate balance of flavors that made a cup of coffee stand out. More than just technical skills, they passed down philosophies about hospitality, work ethic, and the discipline it took to thrive in this craft. Some of the best baristas I worked with had mentors who drilled into them the smallest details, the weight of the portafilter in their hands, the precise moment to stop steaming milk, the subtle cues that signaled when a shot was pulling too fast or too slow.

Despite the depth of skill and dedication required, working as a barista in Singapore still came with an unspoken ceiling.

The Weight of Expectations

Unlike in countries where careers in hospitality are highly respected, Singapore continues to struggle with the perception that working in F&B is temporary, a stepping stone rather than a destination. Parents expect their children to pursue jobs that offer financial security, career progression, and social prestige. A role behind the counter, no matter how skilled, rarely fits that mold.

The best baristas I've trained or worked with have often left the industry. It wasn't because they lacked passion or ability, but because the pressure to move into something more "stable" was always present.

Many pursue academic excellence, civil service jobs, or corporate careers in multinational companies, believing that barista work is something to leave behind once life takes shape. It is often seen as a stopgap, a job that fills the space between degrees, career shifts, or bigger plans. There is an expectation that at some point, anyone serious about their future will step away from the espresso machine and move toward a role that fits the mold of stability and success.

Then there are those who stay, but with the constant pressure to move up quickly. Standing behind the counter for too long can feel like standing still. Some push themselves into management roles as soon as the opportunity arises, whether they are prepared for the responsibility or not. Others transition into roasting or wholesale, believing that handling the business side of coffee is a way to justify staying in the industry. Progress, for them, is measured by how far they can move away from the bar.

Few allow themselves the time to fully master the craft of being a barista, even though it is a skill that takes years to refine. There is an implicit expectation that making coffee should lead to something bigger, as though staying at the counter means being left behind.

Retaining Young Baristas in Coffee

A new challenge has surfaced with the younger generation entering the workforce. Retaining skilled baristas has become harder than ever. Their approach to work is different from those who came before them.

For many, work-life balance, mental health, and personal fulfillment matter as much as the job itself. Unlike those who built their careers in coffee over years of long shifts and endless practice, younger baristas hesitate when faced with the industry's demands. The idea of working late hours, being on their feet all day, and grinding through physically demanding routines makes them question if it is worth it.

Some enter with enthusiasm, drawn by the appeal of café culture, the aesthetics of coffee-making, or the idea of working in an environment that feels social and engaging. The reality of repetition, precision, and patience is something they do not always expect. Some want variety in their work, choosing short-term gigs, pop-ups, or part-time stints instead of committing to one café long enough to grow with it. Others feel the need to see immediate results, making It hard to push through the slow process of refining skills like extraction, sensory training, and latte art.

The passion for coffee is often there, but without strong mentorship, clear career paths, and financial security, it becomes difficult to convince young baristas to stay long enough to reach their full potential.

At the most fundamental level, people's views on careers in food and beverage need to shift. Industry recognition plays a role in changing this perception. The spotlight often falls on baristas who win competitions, those who stand on national or international stages with trophies in hand. Their skill is celebrated, and their achievements are acknowledged. But what about the ones who spend years honing their craft behind the bar and working tirelessly without ever competing? They are the ones serving hundreds of customers daily, pulling consistent shots, refining their milk pours, and passing on their knowledge to new baristas. Their contributions shape the industry just as much, yet they rarely receive the same recognition.

For young talents to believe in a future in coffee, they need to see that mastery comes in different forms. The barista who crafts the perfect flat white for a regular every morning deserves as much respect as the one who wins a latte art championship. The one who trains an entire team, ensuring that each barista understands balance, temperature, and extraction, builds the foundation for quality coffee experiences across cafés. Their impact matters.

For those who stay, who choose to commit to this craft, the rewards go beyond a paycheck. There is an unmatched satisfaction in developing a skill with your own hands, in understanding the details that transform a good cup into a great one. For this culture to thrive, the narrative needs to highlight that being a barista is a profession that requires dedication, technical ability, and an understanding of hospitality. The craft deserves to be seen for what it truly is: something worth pursuing, something worth staying for.

Precision in Every Pour

Now, let's delve into the precision required to thrive in this profession. Mastering the art of coffee demands a careful understanding of every stage of espresso extraction and milk texturing, along with the science behind each step. To achieve the perfect pour, everything, including timing, temperature, pressure, and technique, must come together in perfect harmony.

Baristas use different tools to keep things consistent. Scales make sure the coffee and water measurements are exact. Thermometers ensure milk is steamed to the right temperature for smooth, creamy froth without burning. Pressure gauges help apply the perfect amount of force for great espresso. Each tool helps baristas deliver the perfect cup every time.

Making great coffee is all about precision, from the grind size to the water-to-coffee ratio and even how fast the water flows through the grounds. Take espresso, for example. A standard recipe calls for 20 grams of coffee to produce 40 grams of espresso in just 25 seconds. If anything is off, even just a little, it can throw off the entire flavor. Let it brew too long and the espresso can taste bitter and over-extracted. Cut it short and it might end up weak and disappointing.

These details, which may seem minor to the untrained eye, are what distinguish a professional barista from someone who merely operates a coffee machine. For seasoned baristas, such practices become second nature. They can feel when the grind is a fraction off, or sense when the espresso shot isn't pulling correctly just by the sound or the look of the stream of coffee.

Costing is another essential consideration. The beans, carefully sourced from farms across the world, come with a price that reflects their quality and the labor of those who grew them. The milk, selected for its texture and sweetness, adds another layer of cost. Even the water, the energy powering the machines, and the time spent perfecting each shot all factor into the value of a single cup.

Baristas learn quickly that waste is more than an occasional spill or a shot poured down the drain. Every mistake, whether it's overfilling the portafilter, steaming too much milk, or letting an espresso run too long, translates into lost ingredients and unnecessary costs.

This dedication to detail and discipline is deeply ingrained in many Asian cultures, especially in Japan, where craftsmanship is treated with reverence. Whether it is making sushi, whisking matcha, or brewing coffee, the philosophy remains the same: perfection is a process of refinement, built through repetition and unwavering attention to detail.

Japanese coffee culture, particularly the pour-over method, has influenced how baristas approach their craft today. The slow, deliberate spirals of water, the careful bloom, the controlled extraction, every step demands focus. The tools of the trade, the kettle, the grinder, and the tamper, are essential instruments and extensions of the barista's skill.

The journey to achieve this level of precision is far from straightforward. In the traditional kopi world, measurements were guided by the simple use of spoons, whether it was teaspoons or tablespoons. There was no call for scales, no drive for meticulous measurements, just a steady hand and a well-practiced eye for "eyeballing" the right amounts. This relaxed approach, governed more by intuition than by instruments, stood in stark contrast to the new wave of coffee culture, which demands exacting standards down to the last gram.

I remember my early days of brewing coffee in 2007 with a V60. Back then, precision scales were not part of my toolkit. The recipe depended on the markings on the carafe, and measuring the coffee involved scooping grounds with the spoon provided with the brewer. This was how I measured, not by weight, but by volume, a method far from what we would consider precise today.

Even during my time at Starbucks, where I first learned to brew filter coffee using a French press, the approach was similar. Each press, whether it was a 3-cup, 6-cup, or 8-cup, had its own volume. Coffee was scooped according to a standard recipe, and water was added until it reached a specific line marked on the press. It was all about the volume of water and coffee, not their precise weight. The idea of achieving precision in coffee brewing seemed almost foreign.

Looking back, the shift from volume-based methods to precise measurements shows how much coffee brewing has changed. What once relied on instinct and estimation has become a science, where every gram, every second, and every variable matters.

Baristas learn to measure each coffee dose with care, to adjust grind sizes by the slightest fraction, and to fine-tune water temperature with accuracy. The difference between a good cup and a great one often lies in these details. Over time, the process becomes second nature. The weight of the portafilter, the speed of the espresso flow, the way milk stretches under steam all become signals that guide their adjustments.

I still remember my first time competing at a regional barista competition. The stage was bright under the overhead lights, and the judges sat in front of me, clipboards in hand, carefully watching my every move. My station was perfectly set: my tamper was exactly where I needed it, the grinder was dialed in, and the espresso machine was calibrated to the decimal. I had rehearsed every step, refining my process until the very last minute, but no amount of preparation could fully prepare me. The real test was just about to begin.

My heart was racing, but my hands had to remain steady. The pressure of the competition was unlike anything I had felt before. In the café, even on the busiest mornings, there was always room for small corrections. If a shot pulled too long, I could adjust on the next one. If milk didn't texture right, I could start over. Here, every movement counted.

The first espresso shot ran through, and I watched carefully as the golden stream flowed from the spouts. The timer on my watch ticked down. The extraction had to be within range. Too fast, and the flavors would be thin. Too slow, and it would turn bitter. In those few seconds, the hours of training came together. My mind filtered out the sounds of the audience, the footsteps of the floor judges, the ticking of the clock. Everything narrowed down to the cup in front of me.

Years of training have shown me that this level of precision is a mindset. It is about finding stillness in the middle of chaos, knowing that the real skill is not just in getting every detail right but in being able to do it every single time, no matter the circumstances.

The Competitive Edge

Now, I would like to zoom in further into this competitive edge in the world of baristas. Barista competitions exist in a world of their own. They take everything about coffee and push it to the highest level. Working behind a café counter is about speed, consistency, and keeping up with the fast pace of service. Competitions, however, demand something different. Every shot, every movement, every word spoken on stage must be intentional and precise. Competitors spend months preparing. They source the finest beans, dialing in their roast profiles until every sip is exactly as they imagined. They refine their extractions, adjusting their technique down to the fraction of a second. They practice their routines again and again, knowing that the clock is unforgiving. There is a kind of obsessiveness to it that most people never see. The coffee world moves fast, and for the average customer, a cup is either good or bad. But in competition, coffee is dissected. The aroma, the acidity, the body, the aftertaste—everything is judged with exacting standards.

I have been on both sides of this world. I have felt the rush of standing on stage, delivering a routine I had rehearsed a hundred times. I have also felt the crushing weight of getting it wrong. The first time I competed nationally in 2009, I learned the hard way that preparation does not always mean success. The clock was counting down on my fifteen-minute routine. I had planned for every second, rehearsed each step until it felt like second nature. But somehow, time had slipped away from me. I went over, sixteen minutes and twenty-five seconds to be exact. The moment the timer ran out, I knew what it meant. Disqualified.

I stood there, stunned. All the months of work, the sleepless nights spent refining my routine, the hours perfecting my story and technique; none of it mattered anymore. My mind replayed every misstep, every moment where I could have moved faster or spoken less. The disappointment was immediate, sinking into my chest like a weight I could not shake.

As I packed up my station, I tried to keep my composure, but it was impossible. My emotions caught up with me the moment I stepped into the washroom at Suntec Convention Centre. I set my gear down at the sink, gripping the edges of the counter, staring at my reflection. My hands were still trembling from the adrenaline, my heartbeat loud in my ears. Frustration, exhaustion, and self-doubt collided all at once. I let out a breath I had been holding for too long, and before I could stop myself, I let out a quiet, frustrated cry.

As I stood there sobbing, my breath uneven and my shoulders tense, I suddenly felt a firm arm wrap around me. It was a quiet but steady reassurance, a grounding presence that cut through the storm in my mind.

"It's okay," came a voice behind me.

I turned to see Ross Bright, the late Vice President of the Singapore Coffee Association and Singapore's first World Barista Championship (WBC) judge. His voice carried the weight of experience, but it was gentle, without judgment. He had seen countless baristas step onto that stage, had watched them succeed, and had watched them struggle.

"For a first-timer, you did well," he said, his tone calm and steady. "Your coffee was tasty."

I wanted to believe him, but at that moment, all I could think about was the failure. Ross must have sensed my frustration. He didn't try to diminish it or tell me to move on too quickly. Instead, he gave me something to hold onto.

"Competitions aren't just about how well you brew," he said. "They're about staying calm under pressure. You have to practice until every move is second nature. You need to be able to execute, no matter what happens."

I nodded, but the words didn't fully sink in until much later. At that moment, they were just sentences, something to keep me from completely falling apart. But in the weeks that followed, I found myself replaying that conversation in my head.

I started to see where I had gone wrong, not just in the competition, but in my approach to it. I had obsessed over the technical details, had fine-tuned my espresso and milk textures, had rehearsed my script over and over, but I had never truly trained for the pressure itself. I had practiced in perfect conditions, but competition was never perfect.

Ross had been right. It was about adapting, refining, and staying focused when things didn't go according to plan. It was about learning how to keep your composure when the unexpected happened, how to adjust in real-time without letting frustration take over.

So I went back to the drawing board. I worked harder, but I also worked smarter. I changed how I trained, deliberately adding challenges into my practice sessions, timing myself under more stressful conditions, training with distractions, forcing myself to recover quickly from mistakes instead of letting them throw me off. The following two years, in both 2010 and 2011, I returned to the competition stage. This time, I was prepared for more than just the routine.

Both years, I placed third in the national barista and latte art competitions. It wasn't a first-place win, but standing on that podium, I felt something I hadn't felt before: a sense of control, of knowing that I had grown, that I had learned how to handle the pressure rather than crumble under it.

That hunger to improve, to push beyond my limits, led me to step away from competing in 2012. Instead of focusing on perfecting my own routine, I turned my attention to those standing on the other side of the stage. I took on a new role as a judge. I traveled across Singapore, Malaysia, and Thailand, sitting on panels, evaluating performances, watching baristas put everything they had into their routines. Each competition deepened my understanding of the craft. It was no longer about the experience of being on stage, but about recognizing what made a great performance stand out from a good one.

The following year, I took it even further. I went through the rigorous process of becoming a World Barista Judge. The certification process was nothing short of intense. There were 28 international judges from all over the world, including Malaysia, Indonesia, Thailand, Uganda, Australia, the UK, and the USA. We trained, tested, and refined our ability to assess coffee and execution at the highest level. By the end of it, only seven of us passed. Three were from Singapore, and I was one of them.

It was humbling. To go from a competitor struggling to stay composed under pressure to sitting at a global judging table, watching the world's best baristas push the craft forward, felt like completing an incredible journey. But beyond the title and the certification, what mattered most was what I learned. Judging changed the way I saw competition and, ultimately, the way I saw coffee.

I began to realize that the best baristas created an experience. A great competitor told a story with the coffee they served. Every element of their routine, the way they moved, the way they described flavors, the way they presented each cup, had meaning.

Becoming a world-calibrated judge opened other doors I never expected, leading me to judge competitions across Malaysia, Indonesia, Thailand, and Sri Lanka. Eventually, I took on the role of Head Judge, overseeing performances, fine-tuning my ability to evaluate technical skills, storytelling, the precision, and the passion that separated the good from the exceptional.

One of the most defining moments was contributing to the World Latte Art Championships in Melbourne. It was an entirely different level of competition, where baristas from around the world brought their best to the stage, presenting their coffees with an intensity that was impossible to ignore. These were professionals who had spent months, sometimes years, refining their craft for these few minutes in front of the judges.

Beyond judging, I found myself mentoring and coaching up-and-coming competition baristas, guiding them through the rigorous preparation process, helping them fine-tune their techniques, and shaping the way they approached competition. It focused on learning how to translate that skill into a performance that would leave a lasting impression. I also worked alongside fellow judges, ensuring that we all maintained the highest standards of assessment and continuously sharpening our ability to recognize the best in every cup.

Through it all, a question followed me. It surfaced in casual conversations, in passing comments, and sometimes in the direct, expectant way baristas I had mentored would ask.

"Will you ever compete again?"

For years, I had a clear answer. The plan was simple—judge for a while, gain a deeper understanding of competition from the other side, then return stronger, with sharper insights and a better grasp of what it took to win. But plans have a way of evolving. By 2013, I wasn't just judging locally. I had become a certified World Barista Championship (WBC) judge—one of only 55 coffee professionals in the world to hold that distinction at the time.

The stage I once dreamed of standing on had become the place where I now evaluated the best. Year after year, I watched champions rise, routines evolve, and the global coffee scene push the limits of what was possible. And in those years, I learned. I learned what separated the good from the great. I learned how an espresso shot could tell a story, how a barista's ability to connect with the audience could transform a routine from impressive to unforgettable. I also unlearned. I let go of habits that no longer served me, perspectives that had become rigid, and assumptions that didn't hold up in an industry that was constantly evolving.

And then, I relearned. I rediscovered the heart of competition as a stage for ideas where the best routines involved sharing something meaningful, something that resonated long after the presentation was over. But something else stayed with me.

In the Asia Pacific region, barista competitors were getting younger. When I first stepped onto that stage in 2009, I was 27. When I stepped away at 29, I thought I had time, that I could always come back. But now, at 43, I see how much it has all changed. The new generation of competitors are sharper, faster, and armed with resources that weren't available when I last competed. The game has changed. The industry has moved forward. And so, the question has changed. It's no longer just, "Will you compete again?"

It's, "Can you still compete at 43?" "Do you have the time to juggle running a business, leading a family, and committing to months of intense training?"

Competition demands everything. The training is relentless. The physical and mental toll is real. I know that stepping back onto that stage will call for sacrifice, requiring me to dedicate myself fully to a pursuit that demands more than just skill.

Given all this, one might even ask: why go through months of training, financial strain, and the endless chase for perfection? Why return to a stage that has evolved so much since I last stood on it? Maybe the answer is the same as it has always been. To learn. To unlearn. To relearn. So, will I? That's a question time will answer.

At the same time, I've come to appreciate that the competition circuit is not the only path to mastery. The pursuit of excellence takes many forms, and not every barista is drawn to the spotlight or thrives under the intense pressure of a global stage.

Some baristas find their calling in the café, where consistency and efficiency are key. Their world is one of repeatable perfection, where the challenge is not a single flawless performance but the ability to deliver excellence over and over again. They thrive in the rhythm of service, in the familiarity of regulars, and in the quiet satisfaction of making coffee that people return for.

Competition baristas, on the other hand, operate with a different drive. They are fueled by the challenge, the need to refine every movement, every extraction, every story they tell through their coffee. They push themselves to explore new methods, new origins, and new ways of presenting coffee. The pressure doesn't break them; it sharpens them. They belong to a rare breed of coffee professionals, ones who aren't just satisfied with being good and consistently strive for excellence. They chase after something more, something beyond the routine.

What's fascinating is how competition skills transfer into café operations. The same precision that defines a barista's performance on stage applies just as much behind the counter. A barista who has trained under competition pressure moves with intention, knowing that every second matters. A busy café is its own kind of high-pressure environment. Orders pile up, machines run non-stop, and customers expect a seamless experience. A barista who has learned to perform in a competition setting is better equipped to handle this intensity. They understand how to control their workflow, troubleshoot equipment under stress, and maintain a level of quality no matter how demanding the rush gets.

A competition-level barista also brings the same attention to detail that judges look for on stage into the daily rhythm of the café. The way they adjust their grind size to match changing humidity, calibrate their recipes for consistency, and refine their workflow to improve efficiency are the skills that elevate a café from being good to truly exceptional.

Reflecting on my journey, competitions have shaped how I view coffee, both as a barista and as a business owner. The wins and losses have taught me lessons that go beyond the competition. They've influenced how I train my teams, maintain quality, and encourage a mindset of constant growth.

Competitions push you to be sharper, to focus on every detail, and to keep refining your craft even when no one is watching. They teach you that failure is not the opposite of success but part of the process of getting better. The real takeaway is never the trophy; it's the growth that happens along the way.

Whether behind the counter in a café or standing on a competition stage, the drive to improve is what separates those who excel. The best in the industry are not the ones who settle for what they already know. They are the ones who keep searching for ways to be better, to push the limits of what is possible in coffee.

Faces Behind the Counter

Now, I would like to leave you with glimpses into the human stories of baristas who have pushed their limits and redefined possibilities. These are individuals who started with nothing more than a willingness to learn, working through long shifts, making mistakes, and refining their craft with each cup they served. Many have grown beyond the counter, stepping into roles as café owners, roasters, and educators, shaping the next generation of coffee professionals. Their journeys remind me of my own, built on perseverance, passion, and an unshakable dedication to the craft.

I've seen firsthand how baristas evolve, and few stories reflect this better than Ahmad Zuhaimi. He was one of the earliest hires at Dutch Colony, starting out as a part-time barista, someone still finding his footing in the industry. There was nothing glamorous about the role. He spent hours behind the bar, pulling shots, steaming milk, handling the daily chaos of service. But through every challenge, he kept pushing forward, absorbing everything, treating each shift as an opportunity to improve.

Over time, his commitment became impossible to ignore. He climbed through the ranks, moving from barista to café manager, then into wholesale operations, expanding his understanding of coffee beyond the café floor. Today, he is the General Manager of Dutch Colony, having spent over twelve years growing with the company.

In an industry where turnover is common and many leave looking for more stability, Zuhaimi stayed. His story shows what can happen when passion and perseverance come together. He is a barista who looked past the daily grind and saw the potential for something bigger. Watching him grow has been inspiring, a reminder that coffee is about the people who dedicate themselves to it, building careers, communities, and lasting impact along the way.

Nazrul is another example of what happens when a barista commits to the craft and keeps evolving. He started with us as a barista, much like Zuhaimi, learning the ropes behind the counter, developing his skills one shift at a time. But over the years, his focus began to shift. He wanted to understand what happened before the coffee reached the bar, how flavors were developed, how roasting transformed a green bean into something with depth and character.

Today, after eleven years with us, Nazrul has become our lead coffee roaster, overseeing one of the most critical aspects of our coffee production. His responsibility is far greater; he is the one shaping the flavor profiles that define our coffees. Every batch he roasts sets the foundation for what is served in our cafés, and his precision and expertise ensure that each coffee meets the standards we have worked so hard to build.

Stories like Zuhaimi's and Nazrul's aren't unique to Dutch Colony. Across the industry, baristas have taken their early experiences and used them as stepping stones to something bigger. Some have stayed in the café world, moving into managerial, operational, or educational roles, becoming the backbone of the establishments they helped build.

Some have gone into regional sales, working with equipment manufacturers, bringing their hands-on knowledge of coffee-making into the business side of the industry. Others have stepped into green coffee importing, forging relationships with farmers, understanding the complexities of sourcing, and ensuring that quality coffee reaches roasters and cafés worldwide. There are also those who have become coffee consultants, traveling, training, and guiding businesses in refining their approach to coffee.

I have also seen baristas take their experience and pour it into something of their own, stepping into café ownership and shaping their businesses with the lessons they learned behind the counter. Among them is Terence, a former colleague whose journey is one I have followed with admiration.

Terence and I worked together at Toby's Estate, where he quickly became one of the standout baristas. He had a presence behind the bar, a quiet confidence, a natural instinct for coffee. The way he approached every aspect of the craft with discipline and purpose truly set him apart. It didn't take long for his talent to shine. He started competing and winning, proving that he had what it took to stand among the best.

After leaving Toby's, he went on to work for a larger roaster, deepening his understanding of coffee beyond the café floor. But he wanted more. He had spent years honing his craft, learning the nuances of coffee at every level. Eventually, he took the leap, investing his savings, taking a risk, and starting his own wholesale coffee business. It was a bold move that reflected his hunger, humility, and commitment to the industry.

I still remember a conversation we had in 2014, during a car ride with Terence and his then-girlfriend, Priscilla. At one point, I turned to her and asked when they planned to settle down. Without hesitation, she smiled and said, "When he makes it big in coffee."

That answer was a reflection of the kind of journey so many of us go through, one where passion fuels ambition, where success is not immediate but earned through years of learning, failing, and pushing forward.

Terence has more than fulfilled that promise. Today, he is one of the most recognized names in Singapore's coffee history. His business has flourished, and the boy I once worked alongside behind the bar has become a leader in the industry. He and Priscilla are now married, with a son, having built both a career and a family alongside each other.

Looking at these stories of perseverance and success, it becomes clear that being a barista is the foundation of a journey that can lead to opportunities far beyond the café counter. The skills, passion, and discipline developed through long hours of service, endless practice, and the pursuit of excellence open doors that many do not see at first.

The longevity of baristas like Zuhaimi and Nazrul, who have built careers within a single company, proves that there is a future in coffee for those who are willing to commit to it. Their growth within Dutch Colony, from baristas to leaders, reflects the depth of possibility within this industry. At the same time, there are those like Terence, who have taken their experience and ventured out on their own, carving new paths as entrepreneurs, educators, and pioneers.

These journeys share a common thread: they all began with a simple love for coffee. What started as a job, as a way to make a living, turned into something much greater. Each challenge faced, each lesson learned, became part of the process of growth. A career in coffee is as rich and complex as the drink itself. It is a journey built cup by cup, shift by shift, moment by moment. And for those who embrace it, the possibilities are limitless.

CHAPTER 7

Brewing a Career

My own career in coffee, built cup by cup, has been anything but straightforward. No one ever told me how many hats I would wear in this industry, and even if they had, I wouldn't have believed how heavy each one would feel. From the first moment I stepped behind a coffee bar, I felt something shift. There was an energy to it, a flow that pulled me in. But what I didn't realize at the time was how much it would demand of me and how much it would give in return.

I have moved through the industry in ways I never expected. I have been the barista pushing through the morning rush, sleeves dusted with fine coffee grounds, hands moving on instinct as orders stacked up faster than they could be filled. I have been the trainer watching a new barista struggle with their first milk pour, biting back the urge to correct them too quickly, knowing that learning comes in moments of trial and error. I have been the roaster standing in front of a spinning drum late into the night, inhaling the rich aroma of beans cracking open, adjusting temperatures and airflow, hoping to coax out the perfect flavor. I have been the competitor sweating under stage lights, my heart pounding as I set up my station, the judges watching every movement, my routine rehearsed down to the last second but still vulnerable to the pressure of the moment.

I have been the café manager tackling the controlled chaos of a slammed Sunday morning, the sound of the espresso machine steaming milk blending with the clatter of plates, the hurried footsteps of the service team dodging one another in a space that always feels too small. Customers impatiently tapping their fingers on the counter, watching the barista like a hawk, as if sheer willpower could make their cappuccino appear faster. I have been the sales manager convincing café owners to take a chance on a new roast, answering the same skeptical questions over and over, explaining why this bean, this process, this particular profile is worth the investment.

And then there were the moments in between, the ones that didn't fit neatly into job descriptions but shaped me just the same. Stumbling through a foreign city, trying to find a meal after a long day of training, my tired feet leading me to a small shop selling halal kebabs, the scent of grilled meat and warm pita wrapping around me like comfort. Realizing, as I handed over my last few bills, that this would be dinner for the next few days, and making peace with it.

There were nights when exhaustion weighed heavily on my shoulders, but the job still wasn't done. Early mornings came too soon, with the café doors swinging open before I was even fully awake, fueled only by the same coffee I was about to serve. There were silent nods shared with teammates as we prepared for another rush, a quiet understanding that we were all in it together. It was camaraderie forged in the chaos of back-to-back orders and an endless crowd demanding their breakfast faster than I could spell K-O-P-I. Through every role, through every long shift and unexpected challenge, I found pieces of myself.

Each role came with its own trials too. The long hours stretched on, leaving behind aching feet, sore shoulders, and a fatigue that settled deep into the bones. There was always another order to make, another machine to clean, another customer to serve. Perfection was the goal, but the reality was that no matter how much effort went into crafting the perfect cup, it would be gone in minutes, swallowed, forgotten, replaced by the next one.

The physical exhaustion was one thing. The emotional weight was another. The pressure to maintain consistency, quality, and connection hung over every shift. Each cup had to meet the standard, every customer had to feel valued, and every barista I trained had to leave with the skill and confidence to hold their own behind the counter. There were days when it felt like too much, when the milk wouldn't texture right, when a regular sent back their coffee with a frown, when a new barista struggled despite weeks of practice. It was easy to question if it was worth the relentless pursuit of excellence, to wonder if the effort ever truly paid off.

But coffee never let me go. There were moments that made every hardship disappear, moments that reminded me why I kept coming back. The satisfaction of pulling a perfectly dialed-in shot, watching the espresso drip in slow, golden ribbons, the rich, velvety texture curling into the cup below. The deep, caramel-like aroma rising as the crema settles. Knowing that everything has fallen into place: the grind size, the tamp, the pressure, the extraction time. There's no need to taste it to know it's right.

The sight, the scent, the sound of the espresso machine purring as it finishes the shot, all of it tells me this is balance in its purest form.

The wide-eyed wonder of a customer taking their first sip, cradling the cup as if it holds something unfamiliar yet exciting. The hesitation before that first taste, the slow realization as their eyebrows lift slightly, their lips part, and their head tilts just a little, questioning how coffee, something they've had countless times before, could taste so different, so smooth, so complex. Some take another sip immediately, eager to confirm what they just experienced. Others pause, swirling the liquid gently as if decoding its secrets. And then, the words I have heard many times but never tire of: "This is really good."

The look of triumph on a barista's face, hands still slightly trembling, shoulders lifting in relief as they step back and admire their work. The tulip or heart on the surface of the flat white sits perfectly symmetrical, no shaky edges, no broken patterns, just a smooth, confident pour. They turn, searching for my approval, their voice laced with excitement. "Come, look at this," they say, grinning like they've just solved an impossible puzzle. And in that moment, they have. Because weeks of frustration, shaky pours, failed attempts wiped away in frustration, all of it has led to this one moment, where the milk flows just right, and they finally see what they've been chasing.

The celebration that ripples through the sales team, the unspoken tension breaking as the final handshake is made. Someone claps another on the back. Smiles widen, and the relief is clear. A new café has chosen our beans, placing their trust in us. They believe what we offer is worth standing behind, that our coffee will become part of their story. In an industry built on relationships and small gestures that lead to big commitments, this moment carries real weight.

For every challenge, there were always moments like these waiting on the other side. A moment of clarity. A sip of something beautiful. A lesson in patience. A reminder that no effort was ever truly wasted. It reminded me of a line from the Quran: "Verily, with hardship comes ease."

The pages ahead are about the lessons these roles and moments have taught me, the sacrifices that come with chasing something bigger, the victories that make the struggles worthwhile, and the people who have shaped my journey.

Let's explore these with a nod to the many hats in coffee. To the baristas who dream beyond the machines they work behind, who find joy in the small victories: a perfectly textured milk, a well-balanced espresso, a customer's nod of approval. To the mentors who guide, who pass down everything they know, who watch their trainees stumble, struggle, and then one day get it right. To the café owners who carry the weight of it all, who wake before the sun rises, balancing numbers and nurturing teams, knowing that every decision they make shapes lives. Because in the end, we are serving stories, memories, and legacies, one cup at a time.

The Many Paths in Coffee

When people think of a career in coffee, the image that often comes to mind is a barista standing behind the counter, pulling shot after shot of espresso. But coffee extends far beyond that one role. It is an entire ecosystem of professions, each one shaping the industry in its own way.

Back in 2013, even after fourteen years in this industry, after stepping into roles far beyond the café, after flying to Indonesia one month and Korea the next, working on regional sales, meeting with roasters, and sitting across from café owners discussing business strategies, I still have aunts and uncles at family gatherings casually asking if I'm still 'making coffee.' To them, coffee begins and ends with the barista behind the machine. The thought that it could involve global trade, green coffee sourcing, equipment sales, education, and entrepreneurship never quite crosses their minds.

But coffee is so much more than brewing. Some paths are clear-cut, such as a barista refining their skills and working their way up to café management. Others take time to unfold, requiring years of dedication before their full value is realized.

As I mentioned in previous chapters, where we focused on baristas, I have seen many transition into roasters, sales managers, green coffee buyers, educators, and business owners. Many baristas enter the industry thinking only about the craft, about the rush of pulling a perfect shot, the delicate balance of milk and espresso in a well-poured latte, the satisfaction of creating something beautiful with their hands. The energy of a busy café, the rhythm of service, the familiar faces of regular customers, these are the moments that draw people in, that make standing behind the bar feel less like a job and more like a calling.

But for some, something shifts along the way. The more they work, the more they begin to see beyond the cup itself. They start noticing the way a café functions, how small inefficiencies slow down service, how team morale affects performance, how customer relationships shape the business. They realize that what happens behind the bar is only part of a much bigger picture. Some feel the pull toward leadership, toward the challenge of creating an environment where great coffee can be made every single day, regardless of how busy or chaotic it gets.

I learned this firsthand during my time at Toby's Estate, working alongside some of the best baristas in the industry. It was there, in the middle of those high-pressure shifts, that I saw the true weight of responsibility that came with managing a café. A café is a living, breathing ecosystem, one that needs direction, structure, and a leader who knows how to bring it all together.

Managing a café means making split-second decisions when things go wrong. For example, when the espresso machine suddenly stops working during peak hours, there is no time to hesitate because customers are already waiting and the team is looking to you for the next move. It means handling a difficult customer with patience, knowing that your response sets the tone for the entire team, who are watching and learning from you in real-time. It is knowing when to push a barista to improve, challenging them to perfect their skills, and when to step back, recognizing the signs of exhaustion before it turns into burnout.

It also involves creating systems that allow a café to run like clockwork, where the team works efficiently, the workflow is designed to reduce unnecessary movement, and every person knows their role without second-guessing. The best-run cafés do not rely on luck. They rely on thoughtful planning, a team that moves with purpose, and a leader who knows how to balance speed with quality, pressure with motivation, and structure with creativity.

These lessons taught me so much, and I know I wasn't the only one who grew while working at Toby's Estate. The fast-paced, high-pressure environment shaped Terence, Nizam, and Andy, three other individuals who carried what they learned into vastly different roles. Terence went on to become a business owner, building something of his own from the foundation he laid behind the bar. Andy became a senior service technician, mastering the machines we once relied on daily. Nizam took on the role of bar manager for one of Singapore's biggest coffee brands, leading a team in an industry that demands precision and excellence.

Their stories prove that the lessons learned in café management don't just stay within the four walls of a café. The skills such as leadership, crisis management, attention to detail, and adaptability become stepping stones for bigger roles in the industry.

The Human Side of Coffee

Now, zooming in on some of the challenges that came with these transitions, one of the biggest obstacles I faced as a café manager wasn't keeping the café running efficiently; it was understanding the human side of coffee.

A great manager does more than organize schedules and track inventory. They mentor, motivate, and, sometimes, play the role of a therapist. Behind every barista standing at the espresso machine is a story, a goal, a struggle. Some come in young and eager, stepping into the coffee world for the first time, uncertain but willing to learn. Others arrive with years of experience, their hands steady on the portafilter, but their minds clouded with doubt, unsure of what comes next. Some are naturally talented but lack confidence. Others have drive but struggle with technique. And in between it all, there are those simply trying to make ends meet, working shifts to support their families, to put themselves through school, to find a path forward.

A good café manager recognizes this. They see beyond the apron, beyond the coffee orders, and beyond the rushed exchanges behind the bar. They learn to listen, to encourage, and to push at the right moments and pull back when needed. I've spent countless hours coaching baristas, standing beside them as they fought frustration while learning to perfect their latte art. I've nudged some toward competitions, watching as they hesitated before stepping into the spotlight, then witnessing their confidence grow with each round. For others, my role was simpler: reminding them that coffee could be a career, that they had the potential to build something long-term if they wanted to.

Seeing a barista transform from someone timid and unsure into a skilled professional ready to take on the world was just as rewarding as crafting the perfect cup. The shift didn't happen overnight. It was in the small moments: the way they stopped second-guessing themselves, how their hands moved with more confidence, how they began to trust their instincts behind the bar. Over time, I would notice the subtle changes: the barista who once hesitated before greeting a customer now taking orders with ease, the one who struggled with milk steaming now pouring intricate latte art without thinking twice.

I never expected to find so much meaning in watching others grow, but it changed the way I saw my role. Perhaps the greatest affirmation of this came from my then General Manager at Toby's Estate, Andrew Low. One day, after a particularly grueling shift where everything that could go wrong did, he pulled me aside. He had jumped in to help; his face was exhausted, his shirt slightly crumpled from the long day, but there was something behind his expression that caught me off guard.

"Suhaimi, I was the lucky one," he said. "You taught me a lot about hospitality and how passion and respect for others can overcome any obstacles in coffee."

For a moment, I didn't know how to respond. Here was someone I looked up to, someone who had shaped my own growth as a café manager, telling me that I had, in some way, done the same for him. This made me think about how the best café managers don't just run a business; they build a family.

The Bridge Between Coffee and People

After learning the ropes of managing a café, another key step in the coffee industry is shifting into sales and training. These roles call for a strong technical knowledge of coffee and excellent people skills.

I've seen firsthand how baristas with a knack for communication and a deep understanding of coffee mechanics find their niche in these areas. Many of those I've trained have channeled their on-the-ground experience into regional sales roles for coffee equipment, where their detailed knowledge helps cafés make informed decisions about which espresso machines and grinders will best meet their needs. Their ability to explain complex technical details in simple terms makes them invaluable in a market flooded with options.

Others have found their calling in green coffee buying, a role that connects them directly with the origin of coffee. They work closely with farmers and importers, ensuring that the beans they select not only meet quality standards but also align with ethical sourcing practices. This role requires a delicate balance of knowledge, negotiation skills, and a profound respect for the product and the people who grow it.

A great example of this is Noribsham, who started his coffee journey as a barista and roaster under my guidance. But his path didn't end with mastering the art of coffee-making. With his ambition and sharp understanding of the market, he rose to a prominent role in the industry. Today, he's known as the Sales Magnifico at a leading coffee company, where his decisions on imports and exports shape coffee trends across the region. His deep knowledge of coffee flavors, combined with an understanding of customer needs, makes him an essential part of his company.

These different career paths in coffee, whether in management, sales, or green coffee buying, show how incredibly vast and dynamic the industry is. However, there's another role that's just as important, if not more so: training.

Becoming an educator in coffee entails shaping the next generation of baristas and coffee professionals, nurturing their confidence, resilience, and deeper understanding of the craft. It means recognizing potential in people before they even see it in themselves and guiding them through the frustrations of learning until they are strong enough to stand on their own.

Among all the baristas I've mentored, two stand out in particular: Ian Consulta and Khairullah. Two individuals who couldn't be more different in personality, yet equally gifted in their own ways. Mentoring them was a roller coaster ride full of challenges and breakthroughs, but in the end, the pride of seeing them grow into their potential made every struggle worth it.

Ian had a presence that could command a room the moment he stepped behind the counter. He was confident, experienced, and had a natural charisma that made people listen. Customers gravitated toward him, and colleagues looked to him for guidance. He made barista work look effortless, but when he transitioned into training at Cuppachoice, he faced a challenge he hadn't expected.

Being a great barista didn't automatically make him a great teacher.

"I know coffee," he once told me, frustration evident in his voice. "But how do I make someone else know it the way I do?"

That was his struggle. It was never about knowledge; he had plenty of that. It was about patience, about learning how to break things down for someone who didn't yet speak the language of coffee, about understanding that what came naturally to him wouldn't come naturally to everyone else. Teaching required more than skill; it demanded adaptability, empathy, and the ability to meet students where they were, rather than where he wanted them to be.

It took time, and there were many moments when Ian's frustration got the better of him. But as he kept pushing forward, I watched him change. He learned to slow down, to read the struggles of his students, to find different ways to explain the same concept until it finally clicked. I saw him transform into a trainer who inspired those he taught.

While Ian's path to training involved honing his leadership skills and learning to explain complex coffee ideas clearly, Khairullah's journey took a very different route. Where Ian had an instinctive presence, Khairullah was quieter, more introspective, and deeply analytical. He was the kind of person who paid attention to the smallest details, someone who saw patterns where others saw routine. But unlike Ian, who could command a room effortlessly, Khairullah struggled with being in the spotlight.

When he was promoted to Trainer at Dutch Colony, I could see the doubt in his eyes before he even said a word. He had spent years perfecting his craft behind the bar, fine-tuning his skills until every movement became muscle memory. He understood coffee on a deep level—the science behind extraction, the delicate balance of grind size and water temperature, the precise control needed for every pour. But now, instead of standing behind the espresso machine, he was being asked to stand in front of people and teach.

"I don't think I can do this," he admitted one day. I let his words settle between us. He was facing a fear he had never spoken aloud before. But I knew what he couldn't yet see for himself. He had the ability, he just hadn't found his voice yet. Slowly, he started to grow into the role. He didn't try to imitate the trainers he had learned from before. Instead, he found his own way of teaching. He leaned into his strengths: his creativity, his precision, his ability to explain things visually and methodically. While others relied on words, he used demonstrations, diagrams, and hands-on exercises that made technical concepts easier to grasp.

But growth doesn't come without discomfort. There were moments when I pushed him further than he wanted to go, knowing that he wouldn't step forward unless he had no choice. I remember one particular training session when I saw an opportunity to challenge him. The room was filled with trainees, all waiting for the next part of the lesson. I walked over to him, handed him the mic, and without a word, I stepped away.

I could see panic flicker across his face. His fingers gripped the mic tightly, his shoulders stiffened. He took a slow breath, scanning the room, his mind racing through everything he knew, everything he had prepared.

I knew what he was thinking. Why would you do this to me?

Some of the trainees glanced at me, waiting for me to step in. What they didn't know was that I hadn't really left. I was still there, standing at the back, just far enough away for him to feel like he was on his own.

He hesitated at first. His words came out uneven, his voice quieter than usual. But then, something shifted. He started to focus, not on the fear of being in front of the room, but on what he knew. The knowledge was there, buried beneath the self-doubt, and slowly, it started to rise to the surface. His voice steadied. His explanations became clearer. The tension in his shoulders eased.

I stayed where I was, watching him find his rhythm, letting him step into the moment on his own terms. That was the moment I knew Khairullah would succeed. He had been forced to fend for himself, to find his footing without a safety net. It wasn't easy, and I could see the struggle in his eyes. But growth never happens in comfort, and in that moment, standing in front of a room full of trainees with no one to fall back on, he found his own way forward.

I watched as he slowly became the kind of trainer people trusted. The one they turned to when they wanted to understand coffee beyond the surface. The one who explained things in a way that made the most complex techniques feel accessible. The one who, despite his initial reluctance, had grown into a mentor himself.

Both Ian and Khairullah have since moved on, each carving their own path in the coffee industry. Their journeys took them beyond my mentorship, and though they no longer work under me, I feel an undeniable sense of pride whenever I see them succeed.

This, above all, is why mentorship remains one of the most fulfilling aspects of a career in coffee, where you see someone step into their potential and watch them become the best version of themselves, even when they don't believe they are ready.

The Ultimate Risk and Reward of Entrepreneurship

While mentorship and training shape the next generation of coffee professionals, for many, the journey does not stop at mastering the craft. Some take their experience and knowledge a step further, venturing into entrepreneurship, carving out their own space in the industry, and taking on the ultimate challenge of starting a coffee business.

Stepping into entrepreneurship in coffee is a leap of faith. It requires more than a love for brewing or an understanding of espresso extraction. It demands resilience, business acumen, and the ability to adapt to an industry that is as unpredictable as it is rewarding.

When I co-owned Dutch Colony, I quickly learned that being a café owner meant wearing every hat at once. One moment I was focused on coffee quality and customer experience, the next I was an accountant managing costs, a marketer crafting brand identity, an operations manager solving logistical issues, a trainer guiding baristas, and a problem-solver handling everything from equipment breakdowns to last-minute supplier changes. The reality of running a coffee business is about keeping every aspect of the business alive and thriving, even on the toughest days.

Entrepreneurs in coffee take different paths. Some open cafés, building strong brands around their vision and carving out a niche in a competitive market. Others venture into roasting, refining beans and creating unique flavor profiles that define their company's identity. Some focus on sourcing, building direct trade relationships with farmers to bring ethically and sustainably produced coffee to consumers. Then there are those who enter equipment innovation, developing tools and machinery that enhance the way coffee is brewed, extracted, and served.

Singapore's coffee scene is evolving rapidly, blending its rich coffee heritage with modern specialty trends. The growth has been impressive, with the city experiencing a 20% annual increase in specialty coffee shops, which is a clear sign of the rising demand for high-quality, artisanal coffee experiences. Success in this space is about creating a culture and building a community, a place where people connect over coffee, employees are passionate about the mission, and the brand becomes more than just another neighborhood café.

While the growing appreciation for specialty coffee in Singapore creates opportunities, it also presents serious challenges for those looking to enter the market. The café scene is fiercely competitive, with approximately 700 plus coffee shops spread across the island, each trying to create its own identity. Prime locations come at exorbitant rental costs, making it difficult for new players to establish themselves without deep financial backing.

Those who succeed find ways to stand apart. Some introduce technology-driven solutions such as automated ordering systems, AI-powered recommendations, or precision brewing equipment that enhances consistency and efficiency. Others focus on sustainability by incorporating zero-waste initiatives, ethical sourcing, or environmentally friendly packaging to align with shifting consumer values. Concept is king, and those who build a brand, a story, and a purpose behind their café tend to capture a loyal following.

While we will zoom in on entrepreneurship in the next chapter, I want to take a moment to explore how coffee entrepreneurs are also adapting to changing consumer preferences by rethinking what coffee itself can be.

One of the most fascinating innovations in recent years is the emergence of beanless coffee, which is a response to growing sustainability concerns and the rising costs of traditional coffee farming. The concept may sound unusual, but startups like Prefer are leading the charge by repurposing byproducts from local food industries to create sustainable coffee alternatives.

This shift reflects a deeper movement in the industry. As climate change continues to impact coffee-growing regions, supply chain disruptions and ethical sourcing challenges push businesses to think beyond conventional coffee farming. Forward-thinking entrepreneurs are experimenting with new ways to offer coffee experiences without relying entirely on traditional production methods.

As coffee businesses evolve to meet new challenges, so do the careers within them. The future of coffee careers is expanding, shaped by technology, sustainability, and digital engagement in ways that were unimaginable ten years ago.

The Future of Coffee Careers

Advancements in technology are changing the way we brew, serve, and even grow coffee. Precision espresso machines now automate extraction variables, while AI-driven roasting software improves consistency and refines flavor profiles. These innovations are creating exciting opportunities for engineers, designers, and tech entrepreneurs to revolutionize the coffee industry.

Machines today are smarter, more efficient, and capable of performing tasks that once required highly trained professionals. However, this doesn't mean craftsmanship is being replaced; it's being redefined. The barista of the future won't just be someone serving coffee behind the counter but someone skilled in programming and optimizing these advanced systems, using technology to elevate and enhance the coffee experience rather than replace it.

Sustainability is also changing the way people work in the coffee industry. From reducing carbon footprints and adopting circular economy models to creating eco-friendly packaging, these changes are critical for the future of coffee. With more focus on ethical sourcing, waste reduction, and climate-conscious practices, there's a growing demand for experts in sustainability. I recently read that in larger multinational coffee companies, a sustainability officer can earn between SGD 4,000 to 8,000 per month, depending on their expertise. And this field is only getting bigger.

Green coffee buyers are now prioritizing direct trade and finding ways to cut carbon footprints. Cafés and roasteries are on the lookout for waste management experts to help them implement eco-friendly solutions. Even coffee equipment manufacturers are hiring professionals to design energy-efficient and zero-waste brewing systems.

Besides the focus on sustainability, there is another shift in how coffee brands interact with their potential customers. Online tools are revolutionizing how individuals learn about and experience coffee, through digital courses, virtual events, and subscription boxes that bring it closer to them than ever before. As a result, new career opportunities are emerging for marketing specialists, content creators, and e-commerce experts who know how to reach and engage a global audience.

The direct-to-consumer model is on the rise, with coffee roasters and brands now selling directly to customers through online platforms instead of relying only on cafés and retail stores. As a result, roles like data analysts, digital strategists, and social media managers have become vital to the growth of coffee businesses.

Those who embrace these changes, see beyond traditional roles, and find new ways to contribute will be the ones who shape where coffee goes next.

The Financial Realities of Starting in Coffee

Having explored the many paths within coffee, I feel it's just as important to talk about the financial realities of starting in this industry. Because while coffee careers offer passion, creativity, and growth, they also come with hard truths that many don't talk about. The reality is, this is not an industry that starts off paying well. In Singapore, a junior barista typically earns between SGD 1,800 to SGD 2,100 per month, depending on the café and its reputation. Compared to an entry-level corporate job, that figure may seem discouraging, especially in a city where the cost of living is high.

I have spoken about this before on my blog, about the sacrifices, the self-doubt, and the moments when others questioned the path I chose. Many baristas, at some point, will hear the same remarks.

"You're still making coffee?"

"When are you going to get a real job?"

I remember my own early years behind the counter, working long shifts, managing the constant physical demands, and barely making ends meet. There were times when I asked myself if I had chosen the right path, especially when I saw friends settling into jobs with more stability. But despite the doubts, the pursuit of mastery, the satisfaction of refining a skill, and the simple joy of serving a cup of coffee that made someone's day better kept pulling me back: The truth about coffee is that it rewards those who commit to it. Yet, the biggest misconception about working in coffee is the belief that it's a low-paying job with no real future.

It's easy to dismiss coffee jobs as temporary, financially unrewarding, or unsustainable in the long run. But I have seen enough people prove that idea wrong. As I have reiterated throughout, I've seen baristas rise to become head baristas, café managers, roasters, green buyers, trainers, and consultants, roles that command significantly higher salaries and open doors to opportunities beyond the café floor.

Here's a realistic salary progression for those who stay in the industry and develop their expertise:

- **Junior Barista (0-2 years):** SGD 1,800 – 2,100
- **Senior Barista (2-5 years):** SGD 2,200 – 2,400
- **Head Barista (4-6 years):** SGD 2,500 – 3,000
- **Café Manager (5+ years):** SGD 3,000 – 4,500
- **Coffee Roaster/Green Buyer (3-7 years):** SGD 2,800 – 4,800
- **Trainer/Consultant (6+ years):** SGD 4,000 – 7,500 (+ commission)
- **Sales Manager/General Manager (7+ years):** SGD 4,000 – 8,000 (+ commission)

These numbers show one possible path, but there are many others. Some baristas move into coffee sales, where commissions on equipment or wholesale accounts can push their earnings even higher. Others use their expertise to become entrepreneurs, launching their own cafés, roasteries, or specialty coffee brands.

It is not an easy road, but for those who stay, who keep refining their craft, expanding their knowledge, and taking opportunities as they come, coffee becomes a career that evolves with them.

This kind of evolution does not happen by chance. It happens through learning and upskilling. The difference between stagnation and career advancement is often the willingness to invest in education, practice, and skill development.

I've covered this in the previous chapters: certifications, competitions, and continuous education can open doors. In an industry that places high value on experience, formal training and credentials can truly set professionals apart. Baristas who invest time in earning certifications, competing in championships, or attending specialty courses often advance much faster than those who rely only on hands-on experience.

Take the Specialty Coffee Association (SCA) certifications as an example. Baristas who pursue these credentials gain a deeper understanding of coffee quality, sensory skills, and advanced brewing techniques. More importantly, these certifications demonstrate commitment and expertise, which can lead to better career opportunities and higher salaries.I experienced this firsthand when I became both a World Barista Championship Sensory Judge and an Authorized SCA Trainer (AST) in 2013 and 2017, respectively. That experience expanded my professional network, connected me with global industry leaders, and opened doors I never imagined.

Competitions can be a real game-changer. I've worked with baristas whose careers took off as soon as they placed in regional or international championships. A barista who wins a competition transforms into a brand, an ambassador, and a highly sought-after professional in the industry. The visibility, credibility, and confidence gained through competing have the power to completely reshape a career.

In the end, the professionals who rise are the ones who treat coffee as a craft, not just as a means to a paycheck. They are the ones who constantly seek improvement, challenge themselves, and recognize that every new skill learned is a step toward something greater.

The Highs and Lows of a Coffee Career

Beyond the financial challenges and opportunities for growth, working in coffee is physically and mentally exhausting. The reality of daily café life is rarely glamorous, and the demands extend far beyond the romanticized idea of crafting beautiful latte art or curating the perfect coffee menu.

Long hours standing on hard floors, lifting heavy bags of coffee, handling steaming hot milk, and moving at full speed to keep up with the rush all take a toll. The pressure of speed and precision is relentless, with baristas expected to keep their focus sharp even when the queue stretches out the door.

I have seen baristas develop chronic wrist pain from the repetitive motion of tamping. Roasters inhale coffee dust day after day, leading to respiratory issues. Café managers carry the weight of keeping a business afloat, absorbing the stress of staffing, customer demands, and operational challenges, often at the expense of their mental well-being.

I have lived this firsthand. I remember the days when I would open the café at 6:30 AM, push through the relentless rush, then head straight to the roastery for cupping sessions. The work didn't stop there; some nights were spent training baristas in the academy, wrapping up close to midnight, only to wake up and do it all over again. There were weeks where sleep felt optional, where exhaustion sat like a constant weight on my shoulders.

This kind of intensity isn't sustainable, and I have learned, sometimes through painful experience, that burnout is real. Passion for coffee doesn't protect you from overwork, exhaustion, or the mental strain of pushing too hard for too long. That is why I have made it a mission to talk about work-life harmony, fair wages, and career longevity.

Burnout can be the slow erosion of the passion that first drew someone to coffee. It happens when long hours turn into years of overwork, when the joy of crafting a perfect cup is replaced by the pressure to keep up with endless demand. It happens when baristas and roasters start questioning whether their skills are valued, whether their effort is being recognized, or whether the sacrifices they make are worth it.

I have watched incredibly talented baristas and roasters walk away from the industry. Some of them had the skill, the drive, and the potential to become industry leaders, but they were pushed past their limits before they ever had the chance. They were overworked, underpaid, and left without a clear path for growth. Without the right support, they couldn't see a future in coffee and so they left, taking with them years of experience, talent, and passion that the industry desperately needed.

Thankfully, change is happening. More cafés now recognize that longevity in coffee requires sustainability, not just for the beans but for the people who bring coffee to life. Businesses are prioritizing fair wages, structured schedules, and proper rest periods. Some cafés have introduced five-day work weeks for baristas, while others have profit-sharing models that allow staff to feel invested in the business they help build. Career development programs are becoming more common, providing training beyond the bar so that baristas can move into roles like roasting, management, or coffee education.

At Dutch Colony, I made it a point to train my team to understand that coffee could be a long-term career. That meant mentoring them in career planning, financial literacy, and leadership development, in addition to technical skills.

Of course, this essential support from businesses helps, but staying in the coffee industry for the long run also requires personal strategies to combat burnout and find fulfillment.

One of the most important things is setting boundaries early. It's easy to get caught up in the culture of pushing through exhaustion, but learning when to step back is crucial. Taking breaks, setting realistic schedules, and knowing when to say no can make the difference between lasting in this industry and burning out within a few years.

Finding a support system is equally important. The coffee industry is built on community, and surrounding yourself with people who understand the challenges, whether it's colleagues, mentors, or fellow baristas, can make even the hardest days feel manageable. Having someone to share frustrations with, to celebrate small wins, and to remind you why you started can help keep the passion alive.

It also helps to have a long-term vision. Coffee careers don't always follow a straight path, but having a general direction, whether it's moving into roasting, management, or even opening your own business, gives purpose to the everyday grind.

The key to staying on this path is about finding a way to grow without losing the passion that brought you here in the first place. I won't lie, this industry isn't for everyone. It is tough, it is demanding, and it requires a deep, personal love for coffee that goes beyond making drinks but coffee isn't a dead-end job. It is an industry that gives back what you put into it. But while the long-term rewards are there, the struggle to see the future clearly in the early years is something many baristas go through.

I remember one evening after a long, draining shift when a young barista stopped me as I was about to leave. His uniform was slightly wrinkled, and he nervously fidgeted with the pen in his hand, uncertainty written all over his face.

"I don't know if this is for me," he said quietly. "I love coffee, but I don't see a future in it. Everyone keeps telling me to get a real job."

There was something familiar about his words. I had stood in his place once, feeling the same uncertainty, questioning if I had chosen the right path. I remembered the exhaustion that sank into my bones after twelve-hour shifts, the birthdays and celebrations I had missed because of work, the moments when it felt like I was running on nothing but caffeine and habit.

I looked at him and asked, "If you could strip everything else away, the long hours, the doubts, the external pressure, what is it about coffee that makes you stay?"

He hesitated, his fingers running over the edges of his apron. For a moment, it seemed like he wasn't sure how to answer. Then, finally, he spoke.

"It's the connections," he said. "The way you recognize a regular's order before they even say it. The way a well-made espresso feels like second nature after months of practice. That feeling when you serve someone a coffee and, for a moment, they forget everything else and just enjoy the experience."

I nodded, recognizing the feeling all too well. "Then you're already in deeper than you think," I told him.

I knew that if he could see past the exhaustion and the uncertainty, if he focused on the moments that made him feel alive behind the bar, he would understand that coffee had already become a part of him. I shared with him the stories of others who had once stood where he was, unsure of their path, questioning if they should continue. I told him about Fadhly, whom I had hired years ago. He had started with the same hesitations, wondering whether coffee could be a real career. But step by step, he grew, from barista to roaster, from roaster to green coffee buyer, eventually shaping the way coffee is sourced in Southeast Asia. His work now impacts farmers, importers, and cafés across the region, all because he chose to stay and see where the industry could take him.

Then there was Muhammad Aga, whom I first met at the ASEAN Barista Championship in Thailand back in 2011, who began as a junior barista with no guarantees of where the job would lead. Through years of training, competition, and perseverance, he became an elite barista competitor, a respected figure in Indonesia's coffee scene, and now a mentor to the next generation of coffee professionals. His journey wasn't easy, but he faced every challenge and turned it into an opportunity.

"It's not about whether this is a real job," I told him, watching as he wrestled with his thoughts after hearing these stories. "It's about whether you're willing to make it a real career."

We stayed long after the café closed, the espresso machine quiet for the night, but the faint smell of coffee still hung in the air. We talked about upskilling, about competitions, and I didn't try to convince him to stay. That wasn't my place, and it wasn't my decision to make. What I wanted was for him to understand that coffee, like any craft, gives back what you put into it. It challenges you, tests your patience, and, at times, makes you question everything. But for those who push forward, the rewards are deeper than they ever expect.

He left a few months later to pursue a career in banking. For a while, I wondered if he had found what he was looking for. Maybe he had. Maybe coffee was just a phase, something he would look back on fondly before moving on. A few years passed before I saw him again.

This time, he wasn't standing with uncertainty or doubt. He was behind the bar at a respected specialty café, moving with the rhythm of someone who knew exactly where he belonged. He poured latte art with confidence, chatting easily with customers, the hesitation in his voice replaced by the ease that comes with experience. He caught my eye and grinned, setting down a cappuccino before walking over.

"I get it now," he said, his voice steady. "Thank you."

I smiled, but I didn't need to say anything. In that moment, I felt that deep sense of fulfillment that doesn't come from making the perfect cup, but from helping someone else see their own potential.

This is what life in coffee is truly about. It is about dreams that start small and grow over time. It's about the dedication to learning, the joy that comes with making progress, and the determination to keep going even when the path gets tough. For those who stick with it, put in the effort, and see the bigger picture, coffee becomes something deeper. It becomes a calling.

CHAPTER 8

Ground Up – Building a Coffee Business

My calling in coffee, fueled by many dreams, soon led to something bigger than I had ever imagined. The path I had walked, from standing behind the bar to training baristas, from competing to judging, had all been leading me here. That dream took shape in the form of Dutch Colony Coffee Co., a chance to build something from the ground up where coffee could be experienced in its purest form.

I remember the first time we walked into the space that would become Dutch Colony number 07. It was empty, unfinished, and filled with the sharp smell of fresh cement and sawdust. The floors were raw concrete, the walls stripped bare, exposing layers of history beneath the paint that had once covered them. The place was cold and still, but in my mind, it was already alive.

I could see it: shelves lined with bags of freshly roasted coffee, each one carrying the distinct aroma of beans sourced from different parts of the world. The quiet in the room now would soon give way to the steady buzz of conversation, the gentle clink of cups meeting saucers, and the comforting hiss of milk steaming to perfection. I pictured the first customers walking in, taking a deep breath of the warm, rich scent of fresh coffee, and instantly feeling at home.

Beside me, my partners stood, each lost in their own vision of what this place could become. Despite the hectic nature of our schedules, filled with planning, financial meetings, and endless decision-making, we had made it a point to come together here. It had quickly become our ritual: walking the space, inspecting every corner for defects, running our hands over the cold, rough surfaces of the unfinished walls. It was as if we could absorb the potential of the place through touch.

This act of walking through the space was grounding. It connected us, physically and emotionally, to the project, reminding us that we were building something real, something that would soon take on a life of its own. In those quiet moments, we didn't speak much. Instead, we each offered a silent prayer while walking around the shop, our faith manifesting in our quiet presence. It was an act of belief, not just in the business, but in each other, and in the dream we were building.

Atan broke the silence first, his voice carrying both excitement and nerves. He gestured toward the front of the shop, where a large, empty display case and open space stood. "Can you picture it?" he asked. "The counter will go right there, with the Modbars drawing people in. And over there, a huge DCC lightbox, bright enough to catch the eyes of people on the passing trains."

I nodded and smiled, letting my mind fill in the details. "I can almost hear it, the sound of milk frothing, the door chiming each time someone walks in. It's like listening to the heartbeat of a place that's just starting to come alive."

Meidia, usually the one to keep us grounded, gave a small sigh. "It still feels surreal," she confessed, looking around at the bare walls that would soon pulse with life. "Like we're standing in the middle of a dream that's not quite ready to wake up."

I allowed my mind to shape what wasn't there yet. The first customer stepping in, pausing for just a second before placing their order, hesitant now but eventually this place would feel like home to them. I imagined the laughter of friends catching up in a corner, their voices mixing with the buzz of conversation. Someone working quietly by the window, their fingers tapping against a phone as they sipped a perfectly dialed-in espresso. The occasional burst of excitement from behind the bar when a barista nailed the perfect pour, their pride evident in the way they held up the cup before setting it down.

The thought filled me with energy. But beneath that exhilaration, a quiet fear crept in. Passion had brought us here, but would it be enough? The weight of reality pressed down, heavier than the dust in the air. Every choice suddenly carried more meaning than it had before. The layout of the counter, the way customers would move through the space, the beans we would serve, the music that would fill the room: it all had to come together in a way that made people want to return. Because this was about creating a space where people felt welcome, where they could sit a little longer, where they knew they belonged.

A hand clapped my shoulder, jolting me back to the present. Atan stood beside me, grinning. "Well," he said, "it's time to turn this dream into something real."

And just like that, the work began. Every decision we made, from the way the counter was positioned to the beans we chose to serve, mattered in ways we couldn't afford to overlook. From choosing the espresso machines that would drive our operation to selecting the suppliers for our ingredients, every decision played an important role in shaping our cafe's story. Beyond the romantic vision of coffee shop conversations and the sound of clinking cups, there was the practical side of things: licenses, health regulations, and marketing. Each logistical detail required just as much focus as the quality of our coffee.

As I thought about it all, the task ahead felt huge, but the excitement of turning our vision into reality kept me determined. I took a deep breath and looked at my partners, ready to talk about our next steps. I knew that together we had the passion and drive to turn this empty space into a lively hub of coffee culture. Our journey was officially underway.

From Idea to Reality

This official journey of creating a café is fundamentally about translating an idea, a spark of possibility, into a living, breathing space. Every great café begins as a seed in the mind that, when carefully cared for, blossoms into something much larger than itself.

Starting a café in a lively and busy city like Singapore requires a clear plan and careful execution of the idea. With hundreds of options already lining the streets, the true challenge for a new coffee business is standing out from the rest. Cafés must offer something more meaningful than just quality beverages to attract loyal customers. Some cafés offer a rare sanctuary from the city's relentless pace, wrapping you in a welcoming quiet that feels almost impossible to find amidst the nonstop rush outside. These are spaces designed with care and warmth, with soft lighting, comfy seating, shelves filled with thoughtfully chosen books, and cozy corners that seem to gently encourage you to slow down and stay awhile. Customers step inside, leaving their hurried footsteps at the door, finding comfort in the aroma of freshly ground coffee beans and baked pastries.

Other cafés embrace the city's rhythm and intensity, providing quick espresso-based drinks tailored to busy commuters. These places keep service swift, but they are thoughtful in how they connect with customers. Even in just the few brief minutes it takes to prepare an espresso or cappuccino, baristas manage a friendly chat, remembering faces and favourite orders. For office workers rushing between meetings, these brief interactions offer a moment of warmth amidst their fast-paced lives.

Then, there are the cafés that take a purist approach, treating coffee as an art form. These places focus on perfecting the craft, honoring the bean, and turning the experience into something almost ceremonial. They pride themselves on sourcing single-origin beans, dialing in precise extractions, and mastering every brewing method down to the second. There is no rush here, no shortcuts. Each cup is a conversation starter, a gateway into the world of coffee, where flavor is dissected, discussed, and appreciated. The baristas behind the bar provoke thought, encourage curiosity, and transform coffee drinking from a habit into an experience.

But cafés are more than the coffee they serve. They are about the spaces we create. Some cafés naturally evolve into community hubs, drawing in creatives, students, and freelancers who settle into their favorite corners, turning the space into an extension of their work and their lives. There is an energy to these places, a flow dictated by the people who gather there. Mornings start with quiet focus, as laptops open, notebooks fill with fresh ideas, and coffee cups sit half-drunk beside them. By midday, conversations start flowing, voices overlap, and ideas bounce between strangers who, in any other setting, might never have met. A café like this becomes a part of the heart of the city, a place where lives intersect in unexpected ways.

For these cafés to thrive, they must have a soul, a purpose that extends beyond transactions. They must invite people in and make them want to stay, for the coffee as well as the feeling of belonging. That's why defining the vision early on is so important. Whether the goal is to serve the best pour-over in town, become a go-to brunch spot, or champion sustainability, this decision shapes everything that follows. The vision is the foundation; it dictates the brand identity, the menu, the way customers interact with the space, and the kind of experience they walk away with. Every small detail, from the type of cups used to the layout of the furniture, reflects the bigger picture. Even the choice of location is influenced by this vision. A quiet street corner may lend itself to slow mornings with regulars who bring their books and stay a while. A café at a busy intersection may cater to the hurried city dweller, needing their coffee on the go. A tucked-away spot, hidden from the main roads, might attract those looking for something undiscovered, a space that feels like their own little secret.

Standing in the empty space that would become Dutch Colony, I felt the weight of this realization. We were dreamers, caught up in the thrill of creating something meaningful. But a dream, no matter how strong, needs clarity, direction, and a structure. It needed to be a business that could sustain itself, grow, and adapt. Without that structure, even the best café could fade into the background.

Talking about structure, it's important to recognize that not every coffee business looks the same. There is no one-size-fits-all approach when it comes to building a café. While full-fledged cafés with dine-in service remain the most common model in cities like Singapore, successful entrepreneurs have found creative ways to innovate and redefine what a coffee business can be.

Each model comes with its own opportunities and risks, requiring a delicate balance between ambition, practicality, and the kind of experience you want to create. Let's look at a few different approaches, starting with ***specialty roasteries***.

For specialty roasteries, the heart of the coffee business is in the beans. Roasteries like PPP Coffee and Nylon in Singapore have built their reputations on sourcing, roasting, and supplying high-quality coffee to both retail customers and cafés. These businesses revolve around craftsmanship, education, and precision, elevating coffee from a daily ritual into something that can be studied, appreciated, and understood on a deeper level.

Walking into a specialty roastery, you can often feel the energy in the room. The smell of freshly roasted beans fills the space, blending with its cozy atmosphere. The focus here is on where the coffee comes from, how it's roasted, and the process of brewing. Customers browse shelves stocked with neatly packed bags of beans, labeled with details like altitude, processing method, and flavor notes often compared to wine.

Running a specialty roastery involves storytelling too. The relationships with farmers, the choices behind sourcing, and the deep understanding of how a single bean's journey shapes its final cup are what set these businesses apart. The challenge lies in maintaining consistency by ensuring that every batch is roasted to perfection, customers receive beans at their peak freshness, and both cafés and home brewers are guided on how to get the best out of each origin.

Cultivating customer education is key in this context. It means bringing people into the journey behind their coffee, helping them value every step that turns a simple bean into their morning brew. This takes thoughtful effort; great coffee on its own is rarely enough. It requires a community willing to listen, learn, and value the journey behind their drink. Customers may walk in simply wanting a bag of coffee, but the goal is to help them understand why it tastes the way it does, what makes one origin different from another, and how small details like grind size and brewing time can change everything. That level of engagement turns a purchase into an experience, making people feel like they are part of a movement that goes beyond the usual café culture and into the heart of coffee itself.

For many, running a roastery is an act of love and dedication. It's an ongoing process of refining, teaching, and bridging the gap between those who produce coffee and those who drink it. But while a specialty roastery is one way to shape a coffee business, it's far from the only model that works.

With high rental costs and the challenge of securing prime locations, many coffee entrepreneurs have chosen to go small and go mobile. Instead of investing in a full café, they opt for ***coffee carts and kiosks***, compact setups that allow for greater flexibility, lower overheads, and the ability to move where the demand is highest.

These setups are designed for efficiency. Every inch of space matters, and every movement behind the counter must be intentional. In places like Singapore, where speed and convenience play a huge role in customer behavior, brands like Alchemist and Huggs Coffee have perfected this model. Their sleek, well-designed kiosks serve high-quality coffee to busy professionals in business districts, train stations, and malls, where people don't have time to linger but still want a good cup to get them through the day.

Unlike traditional cafés, where customers may spend an hour nursing a cappuccino, coffee kiosks operate at a much faster pace. Baristas work with precision, pushing out cup after cup in a synchronized flow that allows them to serve as many people as possible. In a high-foot-traffic environment, consistency is crucial. People expect the same quality every single time, and they expect it fast.

But while this model offers flexibility and scalability, it comes with its own set of challenges. The experience is transactional, with little room for deep customer interaction or storytelling. Without the warmth of a café setting, the focus shifts to branding, design, and the ability to create a strong identity within a compact space.

The key to success in this model is efficiency without sacrificing quality. Customers may not have time to chat, but they will return if the coffee is consistently great. And while these setups may not create the same kind of lingering café culture, they become a reliable part of a customer's daily routine, an essential stop before work, a mid-day pick-me-up, a trusted place to refuel amid the rush. The challenge is maintaining the same level of care and quality as a full café while keeping things quick, efficient, and accessible.

It's a delicate balance, ensuring every cup meets the same high standard while serving customers who may only spend seconds at the counter. Yet, for many, this model is the key to reaching a larger audience without the financial burden of a full-scale café.

Beyond traditional cafés and takeaway kiosks, there's another model that has gained traction: ***the hybrid café concept***. This approach blends coffee with other complementary businesses. Walk into one of these spaces, and you'll notice the difference immediately. The aroma of coffee continues to linger in the atmosphere, but the experience goes beyond simply ordering a latte and leaving. Some hybrid cafés include a retail section with beautifully arranged shelves stocked with specialty coffee beans, home brewing equipment, and branded merchandise. Others double as event venues, hosting coffee workshops, industry talks, or creative networking sessions, attracting a diverse crowd beyond the usual café-goers.

There's a natural sense of community in these spaces. You might see a freelancer working on a laptop at one table while a small business owner browses the retail section for coffee-making tools. At another corner, a barista leads a workshop, teaching a small group how to brew the perfect pour-over. The café becomes a meeting point, a learning space, a hub of activity.

Hybrid cafés appeal to a different kind of entrepreneur, someone who sees the potential for coffee to be a gateway into something bigger. They recognize that while coffee brings people in, creating additional ways for them to engage, shop, or learn makes the space even more valuable.

The hybrid model is becoming increasingly popular, especially with the rise of remote work and the demand for flexible workspaces. As more people move away from traditional office environments, cafés that offer a welcoming space to work, collaborate, or attend events are drawing in a new kind of customer who sees the café as an extension of their home or office.

But while this model has its advantages, managing multiple functions under one roof comes with its own challenges. A space that caters to coffee lovers, event organizers, and remote workers needs careful planning and a deep understanding of customer needs. The seating arrangement, noise levels, and overall atmosphere must strike a balance between being inviting, productive, and social. Too much hustle and bustle, and it becomes distracting for those trying to work. Too quiet, and it lacks the energy that makes a café feel alive. The challenge is in creating a space that flows naturally, where different customer groups can coexist without clashing.

A well-structured hybrid café can also help mitigate the risks associated with relying on a single revenue stream. Coffee sales fluctuate, with some days being slower than others. But in a hybrid setup, slower days can be balanced out by event bookings, retail sales, or workshop fees. A café that also serves as a retail space can sell home brewing equipment, exclusive coffee blends, and branded merchandise, offering customers something to take home after their visit.

However, for this model to succeed, the café must offer a unique and memorable experience, something that gives people a reason to choose it over the countless other options available. Whether it's the quality of the coffee, the sense of community, the design of the space, or the opportunities it offers for learning and connection, every detail must feel intentional, not scattered.

Another key aspect is that hybrid cafés compete with more than just other coffee shops. They go up against co-working spaces, bookstores, event venues, and lifestyle hubs. The focus is on adaptability, evolving with customer needs while maintaining the vision that originally made the café unique.

Each business model we have explored presents its own opportunities and challenges, and choosing the right one requires a deep understanding of your goals, your audience, and the kind of experience you want to create. A specialty roastery demands precision and passion for sourcing, roasting, and educating. A high-volume kiosk thrives on speed and efficiency. A hybrid café invites people to stay, work, and interact in ways that go beyond just coffee. What remains constant, though, is the need to be clear on your vision. Whether you're investing in high-end equipment for roasting, building a compact but fast-moving kiosk in a busy business district, or curating a space that blends coffee with retail or co-working, the most important thing is to remain grounded in why you started.

But purpose alone isn't enough. There are no shortcuts. Success in coffee takes ambition, patience, and an understanding of what you're truly offering to your customers. The right business model focuses on how you want your café to be perceived, what role you want it to play in people's lives, and how it will shape the community around it.

The Business Side of Coffee

As we explore these business models, it's just as important to take a closer look at the business side of coffee, because it comes with its own lessons, some inspiring, others difficult.

For many first-time café owners, the hardest realization is this: passion alone won't keep the doors open. I have witnessed many fellow café owners facing this realization, often abruptly. It's easy to believe that a deep love for coffee, the joy of serving it, and the dream of building a welcoming space will be enough to sustain a café. In those early stages, when every decision is fueled by excitement, it feels like nothing could go wrong. You spend hours curating the perfect menu, fine-tuning every element of the café's design, imagining the moment when the first customers step inside and take their seats. The vision feels so vivid, so close to reality, that it's easy to think that pure dedication will carry the business forward.

Then, reality sets in. The numbers start to matter more than the latte art. Rent payments don't wait for foot traffic to pick up. Salaries need to be paid, whether it's a slow month or a busy one. Suddenly, financial planning, supply chain management, and regulatory compliance become just as important as pulling the perfect shot of espresso. The dream of crafting a warm, inviting café must now be balanced with spreadsheets, vendor contracts, and operational costs that dictate survival.

For many, this is the moment when the real test begins. Some adapt quickly, finding ways to balance creativity with business strategy. Others struggle, caught between the romance of the craft and the reality of running a financially sustainable operation. This is why ***understanding the financial fundamentals*** is critical.

The initial investment alone can be substantial, covering rent, renovations, utilities, equipment, inventory, and staff wages. The amount can vary widely, ranging anywhere from $100,000 to over $1 million, depending on location, the scale of the café, and the type of equipment used.

Many entrepreneurs underestimate just how quickly these costs add up. Choosing a prime location may seem like the right move, but high rent can eat into profits before the café even gains momentum. Investing in top-of-the-line espresso machines and grinders is essential for quality but requires a careful balance between ambition and financial reality. Each choice, whether it's the cost of custom-designed furniture, the quality of coffee beans, or the number of full-time employees hired, affects how much runway the business has in its first year.

But while the startup costs are significant, it's the day-to-day financial management that often proves to be the biggest challenge. A café can look successful on the surface with busy tables, long queues, and high daily sales, and still struggle financially. One of the most common pitfalls is cash flow mismanagement. Understanding cash flow statements is one of the most crucial skills a café owner can develop. These reports track how money moves through the business, helping identify potential shortfalls before they become problems. Without this clarity, it's easy to fall into the trap of overspending, assuming that a busy café means financial security. Many café owners learn this the hard way, realizing too late that they needed more working capital to sustain operations through slow months or that they hadn't factored in rising supply costs.

This is where strategic financial decision-making becomes essential. Success comes from knowing when to invest, when to hold back, and how to balance immediate operational needs with long-term sustainability. Beyond large investments, maintaining a financial buffer is one of the smartest things a café owner can do. A contingency fund acts as a safety net, protecting the business from unexpected equipment failures, supply chain disruptions, or seasonal fluctuations in customer traffic.

Managing finances also extends to inventory management, one of the most overlooked yet critical aspects of financial stability. Café owners must walk a fine line between stocking enough to meet demand while avoiding excessive waste. Unlike many retail businesses, coffee shops deal with highly perishable goods. Over-ordering milk, pastries, or fresh produce can lead to unnecessary waste, eating into profits. At the same time, running out of key ingredients during peak hours can lead to lost sales and frustrated customers.

Then, there are the price fluctuations of coffee beans and other essential supplies. Global coffee prices can shift dramatically due to climate conditions, supply chain disruptions, or geopolitical factors. Café owners who don't plan ahead and negotiate stable supplier contracts risk sudden cost increases that can erode profit margins overnight. Smart café operators build strong relationships with suppliers, securing bulk pricing where possible or sourcing from multiple vendors to avoid dependency on a single source.

Pricing strategy is another delicate balance. Set prices too high, and customers may turn elsewhere. Price too low, and profit margins disappear. It's tempting to compete on price, especially when surrounded by other cafés, but undervaluing the product can lead to long-term sustainability issues. Instead, the focus should be on pricing that reflects quality, experience, and brand positioning, ensuring that customers see value in what they are paying for.

The ability to tackle the financial aspects of running a coffee business is crucial, but it's only one piece of the puzzle. To thrive and build lasting success, you also need ***operational efficiency***. It's the backbone of your business, influencing everything from how quickly customers are served to the overall vibe of your café. When operations are well-managed, customers get their coffee quickly, the quality stays consistent, and the café runs like a well-oiled machine. But when things go wrong, such as when stock runs out, orders pile up, or baristas are overwhelmed, the cracks begin to show.

This is where smart inventory management comes in. Automated inventory systems can track stock levels in real-time, send alerts when supplies are running low, and even show usage trends so café owners can adjust orders accordingly. Techniques like First In, First Out (FIFO) ensure that older stock gets used first, keeping ingredients fresh and reducing waste. Regular audits help catch discrepancies, making sure nothing slips through the cracks.

Operational efficiency is also about serving great coffee consistently. In Singapore's competitive coffee scene, quality matters. For cafés looking to stand out, it all starts with picking the right suppliers. Many of the top specialty cafés go beyond basic supplier relationships. They build direct trade partnerships with coffee farmers to get the freshest, most ethically sourced beans. Some also team up with trusted roasters who share their dedication to quality. These relationships are about building a network that reflects the café's values and dedication to quality.

However, the focus on quality goes beyond just the beans. Every aspect of serving coffee matters, from the milk and alternative dairy options to the type of takeaway cups and the efficiency of water filtration systems. Each component needs to be thoughtfully considered and selected based on how it enhances the quality of the beverage and the customer's overall experience.

And today, more than ever, customers are paying attention to where their coffee comes from, how it's produced, and what kind of impact it has on the environment and the people behind it. They are choosing to support businesses that align with their values.

Cafés that prioritize ethical and sustainable sourcing send a message that they care about the industry, the farmers, and the planet. Many specialty coffee shops work directly with farmers or source from ethical roasters, ensuring that the beans they serve are fairly traded and sustainably grown. It is a promise that extends to contributing to a better coffee ecosystem, and customers recognize and appreciate that effort.

However, even with the right suppliers, premium beans, and state-of-the-art equipment, the absence of standardized processes can lead to inconsistencies that affect the customer experience. SOPs ensure that every barista follows the same protocols for brewing, serving, and presentation, eliminating guesswork and variations in quality. Whether it's the way espresso is extracted, how milk is textured, or how a pour-over is executed, these small but essential steps define a café's identity.

But SOPs shouldn't be rigid; they need to evolve. Customer preferences shift, new brewing methods emerge, and the café itself grows. Regularly reviewing and refining these procedures ensures that the café adapts while staying true to its brand identity.

Staff training is equally important in maintaining this consistency. A well-trained team is the difference between an average café and one that feels effortless, welcoming, and professional.

Baristas need to be trained in recipes, equipment handling, and workflow efficiency to ensure smooth operations. But just as important is customer interaction. The way a barista engages with customers, remembers their usual order, or takes the time to explain a coffee's origin adds to the overall experience. Every small interaction shapes the café's reputation.

Cross-training employees in multiple roles enhances flexibility during peak hours, ensuring that the team can handle rush periods without sacrificing quality or service. A barista who understands front-of-house responsibilities or a cashier who knows how to step behind the bar during busy hours keeps the café running smoothly.

Along with technical skills, ongoing professional development helps build a culture of high standards. Internal training, competition coaching, or sending staff for coffee certifications all help strengthen the café's reputation and build long-term employee loyalty.

When we talk about consistency, training, and quality, we're really talking about people. Behind every perfect cup of coffee is a team of baristas and café staff working together to create a positive experience for every customer. That's why how you manage your team matters; it's the heartbeat of your café.

In the café world, keeping good people can be challenging. Employee turnover tends to be high, which makes creating a supportive work environment crucial. Offering fair, competitive wages and incentives goes a long way toward keeping your team happy and motivated. Recognizing good work, through small rewards, acknowledgments in team meetings, or employee-of-the-month programs, helps your staff feel valued. When employees know their efforts matter, they stay longer, enjoy their work more, and the café becomes a warmer, friendlier place to visit.

Scheduling can also affect employee morale in big ways. Nobody wants to feel overworked on busy weekends or underutilized on quieter afternoons. This is where scheduling software helps. By predicting peak periods and adjusting staffing levels accordingly, you can make sure there's enough staff when things get busy, yet avoid the frustration of idle time during slower hours. The key is finding the sweet spot: enough staff to handle busy rushes comfortably without exhausting them or inflating labor costs unnecessarily. Striking this balance keeps the team fresh, energized, and ready to serve.

Staff management directly shapes another vital part of café operations: customer service. Great customer service happens when well-trained employees genuinely enjoy interacting with customers. A barista who greets regular customers by name or remembers their favorite drink makes even a quick morning coffee run feel special.

Loyalty programs and thoughtful conveniences can further enhance a customer's experience. Simple rewards programs, where customers earn free drinks after repeat visits, make people feel appreciated and encourage them to keep returning. Modern cafés also benefit from self-service ordering kiosks or mobile ordering apps, making the buying process quicker and smoother, especially for busy patrons.

But how do cafés keep improving and responding to changing tastes? Customer feedback plays a crucial role here. Providing opportunities for customers to share their thoughts, such as through digital surveys, casual conversations at the register, or suggestion cards placed strategically in the café, allows business owners to understand exactly what customers love and what could be better. Taking feedback seriously and implementing changes quickly signals to customers that their opinions matter, building stronger loyalty and trust.

Ultimately, every great café operation is rooted in the human factor. It's the thoughtful management of the team behind the counter, the careful attention to customer relationships, and the willingness to listen, learn, and adapt.

Building strong customer relationships and good team dynamics are essential for any café's success. But there's another crucial element that often happens behind the scenes:

managing the complex world of regulations. Every café, no matter how big or small, must operate within a framework of laws covering everything from food safety to labor rights, and staying compliant is as important as any other aspect of the business.

It's easy to get caught up in the creative side of running a café, perfecting the menu, designing the space, and building relationships with customers. But regulations cannot be an afterthought. A single overlooked permit, a missed inspection, or an improperly handled tax filing can result in heavy fines or even forced closure.

In a structured market like Singapore, for instance, café owners must tackle strict health and safety codes, zoning laws, waste disposal guidelines, and employment regulations. Failing a food safety inspection could mean temporary suspension, while not securing the correct business licenses could delay opening plans by months.

Tackling this web of rules requires careful planning and a willingness to deal with the less glamorous side of business ownership. Understanding tax obligations, ensuring payroll compliance, and staying updated with labor laws all contribute to the long-term sustainability of the café. While it may not be the most exciting part of the journey, staying ahead of these requirements protects everything you've worked hard to build.

At the end of the day, running a café is a balancing act. Success comes from understanding how to run a business efficiently, how to manage costs, how to tackle regulations, and how to build a workplace where both customers and employees feel valued. Some days, the focus will be on brewing the perfect cup, refining recipes, or experimenting with new flavors. Other days, it will be about payroll, supplier negotiations, tax filings, and cost management. The challenge is knowing when to shift gears, when to step away from the espresso machine and focus on the backend operations that keep the café alive.

Adaptability is what separates those who survive from those who struggle. Successful café owners learn, evolve, and make tough decisions when necessary. There will be times when the dream feels weighed down by logistics, but understanding how to balance creativity with structure is what turns a café into a long-term success.

Learning from Those Who've Done It Right

Sometimes, the best way to truly understand how this balance works is to learn from those who've done it right. In Singapore, there are inspiring stories of businesses that started with modest beginnings and grew into beloved, thriving brands.

Take Nylon Coffee Roasters, for instance. When they first started, they didn't have grand ambitions or flashy advertising campaigns. Instead, Nylon leaned deeply into something straightforward and powerful: honesty. They openly shared stories of where their beans came from, the farmers behind every batch, and the careful roasting process that made each cup special. Every bag of coffee was a conversation. Customers stepped into Nylon's small space and felt welcomed by the warmth of authenticity and openness. Nylon's team talked openly about their sourcing trips, showed pictures of coffee farms, and explained why each bean mattered. This approach created a devoted community around Nylon, people who trusted and appreciated the transparency behind every cup they enjoyed. Nylon proved that you don't need extravagant marketing or a big team; sincerity and commitment can make your café stand out in a crowded market.

Then there's Chye Seng Huat Hardware, a café that took something completely unconventional and turned it into something remarkable. When they first opened, many wondered how a coffee shop could fit into an old industrial hardware store, with metal gates, peeling walls, and a gritty vibe. But the team at Chye Seng Huat saw possibilities where others saw limitations. They embraced the rough charm of the original space, keeping its industrial character intact while introducing specialty coffee. Customers walking through the metal doors instantly felt like they were stepping into something special, a creative blend of past and present. Old metal shelves, wooden tables, and exposed fixtures weren't merely décor; they were a tribute to the building's history, a deliberate choice to offer a completely unique experience. Chye Seng Huat was serving an atmosphere, a sense of discovery, and an appreciation for thoughtfully reimagined spaces.

Kurasu Singapore is another great example. Originally from Kyoto, Kurasu didn't try to change itself to fit into the local market. Instead, it introduced the minimalist Japanese café culture that Kyoto is known for, with clean aesthetics, soft natural lighting, and an almost meditative approach to coffee. The space wasn't cluttered with distractions. There were no excessive decorations or gimmicks. It was all about the purity of the craft, where every movement, from grinding beans to pouring a precise hand brew, felt intentional.

What made Kurasu's approach work was that it attracted the right audience: people who appreciated detail, craftsmanship, and the understated beauty of a well-made cup of coffee. They didn't need loud branding or an elaborate marketing push. Their brand identity spoke for itself. Customers came in because they wanted an experience that felt refined, precise, and deeply connected to the essence of Japanese hospitality. By staying authentic to its roots, Kurasu carved out a unique place in Singapore's coffee scene.

If there's one takeaway from these cafés, it's that success isn't about following trends or trying to appeal to everyone. It's about knowing exactly who you are as a brand and delivering that experience with confidence.

Each of these businesses, Nylon with its transparency, Chye Seng Huat with its immersive atmosphere, and Kurasu with its quiet elegance, thrived because they understood their identity and their customers. But they also recognized another crucial factor: the fundamentals of running a business. They embraced the realities of finance, operations, and customer expectations.

They adapted where needed, but never at the cost of losing what made them unique. That's the key to staying relevant in a fast-changing market. It's not about trying to be everything to everyone. It's about being the best version of what you set out to be.

The Milestone Moments

As you build your café based on these lessons, meaningful layers will continue to emerge. These are the quiet moments that assure you that you are on the right path. They aren't big milestones or grand celebrations, but they carry deep meaning because they confirm that your dream is becoming real.

I vividly remember one particular morning shortly after we opened Dutch Colony. It was quiet, and the baristas were just beginning to get comfortable behind the counter. A customer walked in, glanced around thoughtfully, and, without hesitation, ordered a flat white by scanning the QR code fixed at the corner of the table. He settled into a seat by the window, opened his laptop, and began working. It was simple. But in that brief moment, something changed for me. I realized we had created a space someone genuinely wanted to return to. It was no longer just a space filled with potential; it was now becoming someone's daily spot. It was part of his morning ritual, his moment of comfort before facing the day ahead. This quiet moment told me we were on the right track more clearly than any sales report ever could.

Then came the day when the café first turned a profit. We had spent months worrying over every cent, hoping to reach a break-even point and constantly asking ourselves if we were doing enough. It wasn't a dramatic announcement or an immediate relief. It was simply sitting down at the table after hours, staring at the spreadsheet, seeing the numbers balance out, and realizing, almost with disbelief, that we had finally crossed into profitability. It reassured us that our decisions, our careful spending, and all those sleepless nights had mattered.

But it wasn't all smooth sailing. There were challenges that shook us to the core, doubts that made us question everything. We learned lessons the hard way, making mistakes that would sometimes take weeks or even months to correct. Yet, no matter how difficult things got,me and my partners found our way back to the ritual. Every week, the three of us would stand together in that space, walking through the quiet, empty rooms, checking every corner, inspecting every detail, offering silent prayers to keep us grounded. It was our way of honoring how far we had come, and how far we still had to go.

We knew the road ahead wasn't always going to be smooth. Some weeks, we would see growth and feel like we were getting closer to what we envisioned. Other weeks, we would wrestle with setbacks that made us question whether we had made the right choices. There were days when it felt like we were building something unstoppable, and other days when it felt like we were one wrong step away from losing it all.

But through it all, we reminded ourselves why we had started. As we stood in the quiet of the café before the doors opened for another day, we could still feel that same mix of fear and excitement that had been there at the very beginning. It never left us. It lived in us, in every decision, every late-night brainstorming session, and every quiet moment of reflection.

In those moments, I often found myself reflecting on how our success was never solely about sales figures or recognition. It lived within the bonds we formed with customers, within the growth we saw in our team, and within the simple act of sharing something we truly cared about. We came to see clearly that our café was offering people a place where they felt seen, appreciated, and comfortable enough to pause amid the rush of daily life. It was a place where regular customers became friends, where new visitors were welcomed warmly, and where every sip of coffee was an invitation to be a part of something bigger. We had built something real, something that reached beyond the cups we served. And I felt it then, the certainty that we were exactly where we were meant to be.

CHAPTER 9

Dutch Colony Coffee Co. – Crafting a Dream

I want to share more about the journey that led us to this moment of certainty, the feeling that we had arrived exactly where we belonged. In March 2013, Dutch Colony Coffee Co. was just another name on my client list, a new café in a city already crowded with coffee shops. As a sales manager, I was there simply to provide the machines and equipment they needed. At first, it felt like any other sales meeting. There was paperwork to sort through, orders to fulfill, and logistics to coordinate. But something about this café drew my attention and sparked a quiet curiosity inside me.

The first time I stepped foot in Dutch Colony, it felt oddly isolated, situated deep inside Turf City in Bukit Timah. It was the sort of place you would never stumble upon by chance. Buses ran infrequently, and MRT stops were nowhere close. Getting there required determination, whether it was a long drive or an expensive taxi ride. Yet despite the location, customers seemed willing to make the effort. This baffled me. I had seen cafés struggle in prime locations, let alone an isolated corner hidden within a sleepy commercial space. I wondered what was drawing people to a café so out of the way. My curiosity grew. I found myself returning often, lingering longer each time.

Yet before I fully understood what Dutch Colony would become for me, there was one moment that truly sealed my connection to the brand, a misadventure that still makes me smile every time I recall it. One afternoon, the Operations Manager at the time had given me the address to visit the café for the very first time. Confidently, I punched it into my GPS and headed out. Soon, I found myself pulling into a place that felt off. Instead of coffee shops or familiar café signage, all I saw were horses strolling leisurely around lush green paddocks.

Puzzled, I picked up my phone and called him immediately. “Hey,” I said, confusion clear in my voice, “I think I’m here, but are you sure this is correct? I see horses everywhere.”

"Yes, yes! Turf Club!" he responded confidently.

That was when it clicked. Turf Club and Turf City, two entirely different places but linked by their history in horse racing. I had unknowingly driven straight into the Turf Club, Singapore’s well-known horse racing facility, when I was supposed to be at Turf City, the former Turf Club site now repurposed into a retail and dining hub. The realization sent me into a mix of frustration and amusement. A 30-kilometer detour later, I finally arrived at Dutch Colony, carrying with me a story that immediately became part of my connection with this new brand.

The more time I spent there, the more deeply I became invested. My role evolved naturally, from supplier to informal mentor. The team soon came to expect my visits, greeting me warmly each time I stepped through the doors. I found myself staying later, conversations about coffee spilling into conversations about dreams, aspirations, and ambitions. Slowly, Dutch Colony had started to feel less like a customer and more like something I belonged to, a place I was helping nurture and grow.

When the opportunity arose to become a partner, I didn't hesitate, even though the idea of being a business owner felt daunting and completely unfamiliar. I wasn't fully prepared, but I had big, hairy, audacious goals and a restless eagerness to see what I could achieve.

Eleven years later, standing here, I look around and marvel at how far we've come. Dutch Colony is now a thriving brand, recognized and respected, driven by passion and dedication. Reflecting on how my journey began with that accidental detour to Turf Club and quiet coaching sessions after hours, I realize those moments perfectly capture the essence of this journey. Curiosity turned into passion, guidance grew into mentorship, and dreams slowly but surely transformed into reality.

The Birth of Dutch Colony Coffee Co

This journey of mine, from supplier to partner, leads naturally into how Dutch Colony Coffee Co. came to life. It started from a shared passion and a strong vision—an idea born over countless late-night conversations around cups of coffee, scribbled notes, and hopes whispered into the quiet hours long after everyone else had gone home.

When my partners first spoke of creating Dutch Colony, their vision went far beyond opening a café. They dreamed of sparking conversations, creating connections, and fostering deeper appreciation for coffee's journey. Everything they envisioned revolved around authenticity and purpose.

Their initial days were filled with endless discussions about this narrative. I recall watching them sitting together at a small wooden table, papers and sketches spread everywhere, late afternoon sun streaming softly through the shop's zinc sheeted roof. Cups of cooling coffee sat forgotten as they talked passionately about sourcing, roasting, and the ethics they wanted the brand to embody. They discussed how to share the stories of farmers whose lives were deeply connected to the coffee beans they harvested, how to convey the importance of sustainability to customers, and how to create a warm and welcoming atmosphere. Every detail mattered, from sourcing and roasting to the design of the café itself.

The name itself was one of those carefully considered choices. At first glance, the name was met with confusion. People wondered why we'd reference colonial history, especially with its complicated associations. Some questioned if it was appropriate or sensitive. But this was precisely why the choice mattered. It was meant to start conversations, to encourage customers to think deeper about the roots of the coffee they drank.

The Dutch had played a major role in coffee's global history, introducing coffee cultivation to Java and setting up trade routes that helped coffee reach the world. There was no denying that influence, and it was an important part of the story. For my partners, the connection was personal. Coming from Indonesia, they carried the history of their homeland with them. This was their way of acknowledging that history while reclaiming the narrative through craftsmanship, innovation, and community. They saw it as a way to tell a story, not from the perspective of the colonizers but from the perspective of those who had grown up in a land shaped by that past.

When I asked my co-partner Atan what the name Dutch Colony meant to him, he paused thoughtfully before responding. He told me it was a chance to build something meaningful, something deeper than coffee itself. He spoke about wanting our café to be a place that would enrich the lives of everyone it touched, the baristas behind the counter, the customers who walked through our doors each day, and the broader community we became part of. I remember clearly how he explained it, his voice calm yet filled with genuine sincerity. "We started this company and chose this name because we want to use this as a way to bless those around us," he said gently. "We want the team we build here to grow with us, we want our customers to leave happier than when they arrived, and we want the community to feel that we're truly part of them."

That conversation has stayed close to my heart ever since. Every decision we made from then on echoed that purpose: to be part of people's lives in a real and meaningful way. With the name and vision in place, attention shifted naturally toward the core of everything: the coffee. At the time, specialty coffee in Singapore was a small world, still mostly filled with big international brands or a handful of dedicated but relatively unknown local roasters. We understood clearly that Dutch Colony had to find its own unique identity. Branding alone wasn't enough to set us apart. There had to be a genuine commitment to the quality of every single cup we served, from how we sourced beans to how each shot of espresso was carefully extracted.

This clarity shaped how we approached coffee from the start. While some cafés focused on picture-perfect latte art or crafted spaces catering specifically to a niche group, our vision was simpler yet ambitious. We wanted specialty coffee to feel approachable for everyone. From serious coffee enthusiasts who understood the subtle intricacies of extraction to the everyday coffee drinker stepping out of their comfort zone for the first time, our café aimed to welcome them all equally.

We didn't want specialty coffee to feel intimidating or exclusive. Instead, we wanted it to be inviting, inclusive, and easily accessible. This meant choosing coffees thoughtfully, keeping in mind the range of people who walked through our doors every day. For every carefully sourced Ethiopian single-origin coffee bursting with berry notes, we offered a comforting, familiar blend that reminded customers of what first drew them to coffee in the first place. It was important to us that no one ever felt overwhelmed or unwelcome.

Our commitment to differentiation also meant carefully sourcing coffees, always looking deeper than the quality of beans alone. Each coffee we selected carried its own unique story. Sometimes, it came straight from farms through trusted relationships we had nurtured over years, long before sustainability became a mainstream topic. We were committed to ethical sourcing and fair trade practices, ensuring farmers were treated fairly. Other times, we partnered with dependable importers who understood our high standards for quality and transparency. Our dedication to transparency was ingrained in every step of our supply chain, from choosing green beans to the final pour. Every bag we served was chosen because it represented something meaningful, whether it was the farmer's tireless effort, the exceptional care in processing, or the journey that brought the beans to our doorstep.

We wanted these stories to reach our customers too. To do this, we introduced regular Public Cupping sessions every month. The first session was particularly memorable. A quiet Saturday afternoon transformed our café into a gathering of curious faces and friendly conversations. Customers, both regulars and newcomers, crowded around tables laid out with coffee cups and spoons, eager to experience something new. As they sipped each coffee, I guided them through the flavors, sharing the nuances of origin, roasting style, and processing methods. Seeing their expressions shift from uncertainty to intrigue and finally delight was deeply rewarding.

Alongside cupping sessions, we also opened our roastery doors every quarter, inviting the public to tour our facility. Many visitors walked in uncertain what to expect, yet curious about the process behind their daily cup. The sound of coffee beans tumbling gently inside the drum roaster, the warm, toasty aroma filling the air, and the look of amazement as guests saw firsthand how beans transformed from pale green to rich shades of brown created connections beyond the transactional. People left these tours understanding coffee a little better and feeling closer to the brand.

By bringing specialty coffee into everyday life, we created meaningful connections and gradually built a loyal customer base.

The Roasting Philosophy

Central to these connections was our roasting philosophy. From the beginning, roasting meant more than just turning raw green coffee into drinkable beans. We focused on uncovering the hidden potential of each origin, carefully and consistently drawing out unique flavors in every batch. Our goal was to create a taste customers could instantly identify as Dutch Colony: balanced, distinctive, and adaptable as trends and preferences changed.

Finding that balance took countless hours of experimenting, tasting, and fine-tuning. Each origin had something special, something delicate that needed to be coaxed out gently. Every roast profile was treated with care, as we patiently explored different temperatures, roast times, and techniques to reveal exactly the right notes.

Choosing the right roasting equipment was just as important. From the earliest days, we set our sights on using hot air roasting technology. This approach provided precise control over heat, giving us greater accuracy and consistency. It also aligned with our values, as hot air roasting reduced energy consumption and environmental impact. We had dreamed from day one about having the Loring Kestrel, a roaster known for its precision, environmental efficiency, and gentle roasting process. But in those early years, with budgets limited and financial realities hitting hard, that dream was beyond our reach.

Instead, we began our journey with the Bühler Roastmaster, a sturdy and reliable machine that was within our budget. It was smaller, simpler, and far more practical for our modest beginnings. But it was still a true workhorse. I remember the nights spent beside the Bühler, its drum rotating steadily, beans inside transforming from pale green to golden brown, aromas drifting through our tiny roastery.

Years passed, our skills deepened, and our brand began to grow. Finally, after six long years, we were able to invest in the dream roaster, the Loring Kestrel. It felt like an important milestone, a validation of all those late nights and early mornings spent by the Bühler. Today, the Loring is the heart of our roasting operation, handling most of our coffee. Its quiet efficiency, precision control, and sustainable operation reflect everything we value.

Yet even now, the Bühler Roastmaster still plays its part. It's a comforting reminder of our roots, and we keep it running both for sentimentality and because it excels at producing deeper, more traditional roasts that many of our customers still seek.

Over time, we refined our craft in developing flavors through roasting. This led us to one of the most defining aspects of our roasting philosophy: post-blending. Many roasters pre-blend their coffees before roasting, combining different origins into a single batch before applying heat. We chose a different path. By roasting each origin separately, we could coax out its individual peak flavors, highlighting its unique characteristics before blending. This level of control allowed us to maintain clarity in the cup, ensuring that no single component was overshadowed or lost in the process. Each origin brought something unique to the table, such as bright acidity, a smooth body, and a lingering sweetness, working together in harmony rather than being confined to a single roast profile.

Beyond the blending approach, our roasting style was guided by one core belief: coffee should taste like where it comes from. We leaned toward lighter roasts, allowing the beans to express their natural flavors rather than masking them with roast-heavy characteristics. We wanted drinkers to taste the bright citrus of a washed Ethiopian, the deep chocolate of a well-processed Brazilian, or the floral elegance of a Panama Gesha without interference.

Of course, lighter roasting demanded an even greater level of precision. Every adjustment to temperature, airflow, and development time could make or break a batch. Too light, and the coffee risked tasting sour or underdeveloped. Too much heat, and the sweetness we worked so hard to preserve could be overpowered by harsh acidity. Roasting this way required patience, knowledge, and understanding how to bring out the best in every bean.

To keep things dynamic, we structured our coffee program to introduce three new filter offerings and two rotating espresso options every month. This ensured that customers had something fresh and exciting to look forward to with every visit. Some coffees stayed on the menu for a little longer, becoming customer favorites, while others came and went in short seasonal bursts.

By 2024, this approach had expanded significantly. We had launched 31 new single-origin coffees and six blends, sourcing from nine different countries. The sheer scale of this sourcing strategy kept us at the forefront of Singapore's specialty coffee scene. More importantly, it kept us engaged. Roasting was never static; it was always evolving, always teaching us something new.

For a relatively young roasting company in Asia, the road we have traveled has been nothing short of remarkable.

Every milestone we've achieved is a reflection of our team's dedication and the trust our customers have placed in us. In 2024 alone, we roasted nearly 50 tonnes of coffee on the Loring Kestrel, a number that reflects the relationships we've built, the roastery sessions spent fine-tuning profiles, and the cups of coffee enjoyed by customers who have become part of our journey.

But the true mark of progress has always been about refinement, continuously learning, listening, and improving. And nothing embodies this better than the evolution of our Dutch Blend. When we first created the Dutch Blend, we aimed to craft a blend complex enough to intrigue seasoned coffee lovers yet approachable enough for those accustomed to traditional comfort flavors.

The original blend was crafted using four distinct origins: Colombia, Brazil, Ethiopia, and Sumatra. Each played a crucial role in the cup. The Brazilian beans provided a nutty, chocolatey foundation with a smooth, rounded body. Colombian beans brought balance with mild fruitiness and a crisp structure. Ethiopian coffee introduced bright acidity and floral complexity, while Sumatran beans deepened the blend with earthy, full-bodied richness. Together, these origins created a cup that was both familiar and exciting.

As time went on, we noticed a shift. Our customers were becoming more receptive to the bright, fruit-forward flavors of Ethiopian coffees. Their palates were evolving, and so was our approach to blending. We gradually fine-tuned the Dutch Blend.

The first major change came when we removed the Sumatra component. While it had originally provided depth and a heavier body, we found that its earthy, low-acid profile was holding back the brightness we wanted to bring forward. Next, the Colombian component was phased out, making way for a more expressive balance of flavors.

Today, the Dutch Blend stands with a 50-25-25 ratio: 50% Brazil, which provides its signature chocolate and nutty backbone, complemented by two Ethiopian single origins at 25% each. The Ethiopian components introduce layers of floral aromatics, citrus brightness, and delicate sweetness, creating a profile that is balanced yet vibrant.

This shift was about guiding our customers through a journey, challenging and educating palates in a way that felt natural. By making subtle adjustments over time, we were able to introduce a new level of complexity while ensuring that the coffee remained approachable. It became a coffee that encouraged drinkers to explore flavors they may not have noticed before.

The results spoke for themselves. The Dutch Blend earned multiple roasting awards in Melbourne, Australia (2015-2020) and was even used in the winning routine of the 2018 Sri Lanka National Barista Championship. These achievements were deeply validating, but more importantly, they reinforced our belief in pushing boundaries while honoring the integrity of each coffee we worked with.

In this journey of never settling and letting the coffee speak for itself, the real challenge has always been innovation. The world of coffee is in perpetual motion, shaped by changing tastes, new brewing techniques, and deeper conversations around sustainability. From the beginning, we knew that staying relevant meant embracing both innovation and tradition.

We spent countless hours studying global brewing trends, experimenting with new methods, and refining every part of the coffee experience. From fine-tuning our espresso extractions to rethinking hand-brewing techniques and exploring processing innovations at origin, every step was deliberate. Instead of blindly following trends, we aimed to contribute and shape the specialty coffee culture in Singapore and beyond.

Innovation extended to sustainability, efficiency, and our responsibility as a business. Coffee, after all, is an industry that depends on the environment, and we knew that as we grew, so did our impact. In collaboration with SIT University in Singapore, we conducted studies to measure our energy efficiency, looking at ways to optimize our roasting operations without compromising quality. We didn't stop there. We performed carbon emission calculations, identifying key areas of waste and implementing practical solutions to reduce our footprint. It focused on making small, meaningful changes by switching to energy-efficient roasters, optimizing our roasting schedules to reduce excess energy consumption, and ensuring that waste from the process was minimized at every level.

Through Enterprise Singapore (ESG), we took this even further by launching a productivity efficiency project. Growth can sometimes come at the cost of agility, and we wanted to ensure that every expansion, whether a new store, a larger roasting facility, or scaling our wholesale operations, was built on smart, responsible foundations. This project allowed us to streamline processes, reduce operational bottlenecks, and ensure that our standards, processes, and practices align with the best global benchmarks. This balance, of staying true to our identity while continuously innovating, is what has propelled Dutch Colony Coffee Co. forward.

A Catalyst for Coffee Education and Community

This commitment to growth and improvement naturally guided us towards education. We wanted to share our knowledge, pass on our passion, and help others find their footing in coffee, just as we had. That's how the idea for the Dutch Colony Coffee Co.'s educational platform, the Kurasu Coffee Academy (later rebranded as Kurasu Coffee School), first took shape in 2015.

Walking into our training space, you're welcomed by the rich aroma of freshly ground coffee and the faint sweetness of steamed milk. The room buzzes with students exchanging tips and techniques. Espresso machines line one wall, gleaming under warm lights, while pour-over setups and scales sit ready, a nod to precision and focus.

In the center of the room, a trainer is always demonstrating, patiently explaining each step in detail. Training here focuses on building a deep connection with every student, recognizing their unique strengths, and discovering ways to guide them forward. It emphasizes the moment someone achieves a clean espresso extraction, sharing their quiet excitement as they taste the clarity and depth they've created with their own hands.

The academy was created to welcome a diverse group of learners, from beginners curious about specialty coffee to experienced baristas looking to sharpen their craft. With thoughtfully designed classes on sensory training, roasting basics, latte art, and advanced espresso techniques, the academy aims to build confidence, professionalism, and inspire students to see coffee as a career full of growth opportunities.

Our baristas benefited immensely from this investment. From the moment a new hire walks through our doors, their learning journey is carefully structured to ensure that they gain technical skills and absorb the deeper values of craftsmanship, hospitality, and leadership.

The learning begins with a two-day induction program, where new hires are introduced to the very essence of Dutch Colony. They dive into our company's history, the vision of the founders, and our mission of delivering exceptional customer experiences. This is where they begin to understand that making coffee is about upholding a philosophy of craftsmanship, hospitality, and consistency.

During these first few days, they also get a crash course in the fundamentals of specialty coffee, learning about bean origins, processing methods, and the importance of precision in brewing. While they may not yet be expected to perfect a pour-over or pull an immaculate shot of espresso, this initial phase gives them the foundation to appreciate why we do what we do.

Over the next six to twelve months, baristas go through an incremental learning path. This approach ensures that no one is thrown into the deep end. Instead, each barista progresses at a steady pace, building confidence along the way.

- **Induction Program 201**: This advanced module takes what they learned in their first week and expands on it. Here, they begin refining their brewing skills, mastering espresso extractions, perfecting milk steaming techniques, and learning how to maintain consistency during peak hours.

- **Induction Program 301**: By the one-year mark, they enter a more intensive phase, designed to sharpen their technical abilities and prepare them for more responsibilities. At this stage, they work closely with senior baristas, gaining hands-on experience with recipe development, workflow management, and troubleshooting common issues in coffee preparation.

For those who show strong leadership potential, the Head Barista Program offers a path to greater responsibility. Moving into this role is about more than perfecting coffee-making skills—it's about learning to manage a team, ensure operational efficiency, and create an experience that keeps customers coming back. It's about stepping up when the café is at its busiest, making decisions under pressure, and leading by example.

To help them succeed, we offer one-on-one coaching and mentoring from the owners, providing insights into business operations and leadership strategies. They go through hands-on operational management training, where they learn to optimize workflow, control costs, manage inventory, and refine processes that keep the café running smoothly. Leadership workshops help them develop the communication and management skills they need to handle the daily challenges of overseeing a team. And because maintaining a safe and clean environment is as important as making great coffee, they receive specialized training in hygiene and safety audits, ensuring that high standards are upheld at all times.

But training and development are not just about structured programs. Growth happens in the small, quiet moments, the shared doubts, and the everyday experiences that shape confidence over time. It happens in moments like the one I shared with Gavin, one of our baristas, after closing time.

The café had emptied out for the night, leaving behind the sound of the espresso grinder being cleaned. I was sitting at a high table in the corner, sipping our carbonated cold brew from a bottle. I was reflecting on how far we had come when one of our baristas, Gavin, approached hesitantly. He was clearly debating whether to speak.

"Boss, do you ever feel like you're not good enough?" he finally asked.

I looked up, surprised. "All the time," I admitted with a small smile. "Why do you ask?"

He sighed and sat down. "I don't know... I see you, I see the senior team, and you all seem so confident. Meanwhile, I keep second-guessing myself. Today, I messed up a pour-over for a regular. I felt like I let the whole team down. I wonder if I made the wrong move switching from the bar to coffee."

I leaned forward, setting my bottle aside. "Gavin, let me tell you something. A few years ago, I walked into a tiny 400-square-foot space at Pasarbella. I wasn't an owner, I wasn't even part of the company. I was just a sales manager for another brand, trying to do my job. I had no idea that one day I'd be here, leading a team like this. And every step of the way, I had doubts."

He frowned. "You? But you co-own all this."

I chuckled. "No, Gavin. We own this. Dutch Colony wasn't built on one person's confidence. It was built by people who lifted each other up. That's what empowerment means. You're going to make mistakes. We all do. But that's how we grow."

He nodded slowly. "I guess I never thought about it like that."

I patted his shoulder. "You're already better than you think. And the best part? You're surrounded by people who want to see you succeed. You don't have to do it alone."

He smiled, adjusting his apron. "Thanks, boss. I needed to hear that."

As he got up to finish his closing duties, I sat back and looked around the empty café, thinking about how growth is never a straight path. It is built on doubt, struggle, and perseverance. True empowerment entails learning to move forward despite the doubts. That's the kind of leadership we strive for at Dutch Colony. We have always believed in what business leader Jack Welch once said: "The greatest gift of leadership is to develop others to the point they don't need you." That, more than anything else, is what we are building.

This belief is why we go beyond structured leadership development. Continuous education remains a core part of our culture. All baristas, regardless of their role, are encouraged to attend any Katalyst Coffee Academy (KCA) workshop at no cost. These workshops provide an opportunity to deepen their expertise, covering everything from sensory analysis and advanced brewing techniques to latte art and competition training. By creating a culture where learning never stops, we empower our team to constantly refine their craft, stay engaged with the evolving coffee industry, and take pride in every cup they serve.

Bridging Knowledge and Passion

Beyond our internal training programs, Dutch Colony Coffee Co. has always believed that coffee education should extend beyond our own walls. Since our inception in 2013, we have been committed to spreading knowledge and deepening appreciation for specialty coffee. We have seen how education can transform the way people experience coffee. Learning about the journey of a bean from farm to cup can elevate a routine habit into a moment of genuine appreciation.

Through the Katalyst Coffee Academy (KCA), we have built a space where learning is accessible to everyone, from aspiring baristas looking to master their craft to casual coffee lovers who simply want to brew a better cup at home. One of the key pillars of our educational efforts is the globally recognized Specialty Coffee Association (SCA) Coffee Skills Program. This comprehensive curriculum provides learning across different disciplines, covering Barista Skills, Brewing, Green Coffee, Roasting, and Sensory Skills. The program caters to various levels of expertise, ensuring that whether someone is new to coffee or an industry professional refining their knowledge, they walk away with practical insights, hands-on experience, and a deeper connection to the craft.

However, we also wanted to make learning about coffee fun, engaging, and inclusive, even for those who had never considered stepping behind an espresso machine. This led us to develop a variety of corporate and team-building workshops, designed to use coffee as a tool for connection, creativity, and collaboration. These sessions have grown into one of our most popular offerings, bringing people together through the shared experience of brewing, tasting, and experimenting with coffee in a way that feels approachable and interactive.

Over the years, we have had the privilege of working with government statutory boards, multinational corporations (MNCs), small and medium-sized enterprises (SMEs), and private organizations, designing workshops that cater to different group sizes and objectives. Some sessions are intimate, bringing together just ten participants for a focused and immersive experience, while others are large-scale events, hosting up to a hundred people in a single session.

Among the many workshops we have conducted, some stand out as particularly memorable. The Coffee Face Scrub Making session introduces sustainability in a fun and hands-on way, allowing participants to repurpose used coffee grounds into natural skincare products. It is always fascinating to watch participants realize that the coffee they once discarded can have a second life, leading to conversations about reducing waste and reimagining sustainability in everyday habits.

Another favorite is the DIY Espresso Blend workshop, where participants take on the role of a roaster, experimenting with different beans to craft their own unique espresso blend. There is a sense of pride in watching someone discover the balance between body, acidity, and sweetness, adjusting ratios and testing flavors until they create something that is truly their own. The Craft Your Own Coffee Mocktail session brings an unexpected twist, blending coffee with unconventional flavors to create refreshing, layered drinks. Some of the most surprising combinations, like espresso with citrus and tonic, have sparked curiosity and encouraged participants to see coffee as an evolving, versatile ingredient rather than a fixed routine.

For those with a passion for pairing flavors, the Coffee and Chocolate Pairing session is always a hit. Watching people take slow, thoughtful sips of coffee alongside artisanal chocolate, picking up the way different origins complement or contrast each other, is a reminder that coffee appreciation is as much about storytelling and sensory discovery as it is about technique. Similarly, the Coffee & Tea Appreciation session is a bridge between two worlds, catering to both coffee lovers and tea enthusiasts by exploring the depth, complexity, and rituals behind each beverage.

These workshops have created moments: a group of strangers laughing over a coffee mocktail experiment, a team exchanging ideas while crafting their own espresso blend, a first-time specialty coffee drinker taking a slow, thoughtful sip and realizing coffee can be something more. These are the experiences that stay with people, the ones that turn a casual café visit into something memorable.

Fueled by this philosophy, our cafés have naturally evolved into dynamic community spaces, where ideas flow as freely as the coffee. Product launches and brand collaborations have become a regular feature, where we partner with like-minded businesses and creators to introduce new products in a setting that is both engaging and experience-driven. Whether it's unveiling a new blend or hosting a tasting session for an artisanal product, these events allow customers to be a part of the process, to experience something fresh, and to engage with brands in a more personal way.

We have also seen the beautiful intersection of coffee and movement. Running clubs and wellness gatherings have found a home in our cafés, where post-run coffee sessions turn into moments of camaraderie. There is something special about watching a group return, flushed from a morning run, settling into their favorite spots with a cup of coffee in hand, sharing stories from the road.

We have opened our doors to book readings and creative meetups, welcoming authors, poets, and artists who bring their words and ideas to life within our walls. From intimate poetry readings to spirited book discussions, these events have transformed our spaces into havens for those who appreciate literature, art, and the power of human expression.

Our passion for coffee culture has also found a competitive and high-energy outlet through barista jams and latte art throwdowns. These events bring together baristas from across Singapore, turning an ordinary evening into a celebration of skill, technique, and creative flair. The excitement builds as competitors step up to the machines, hands steady, eyes focused, steam wands hissing in the background. The energy is infectious as spectators cheer, judges deliberate, and in those moments, the love for coffee becomes something electric, shared by everyone in the room.

Over time, our venues also witness the personal milestones that touch our hearts. We've seen love stories unfold here, with baby showers filling our cafés with warmth and wedding solemnizations turning our intimate corners into places where vows are exchanged and new beginnings are celebrated. There is something deeply moving about witnessing a couple choose our space for such an important moment, the quiet sound of espresso machines in the background as friends and family gather, laughter mingling with the clinking of cups.

Our cafés have also found their way into television productions and media shoots, becoming part of larger narratives that extend beyond our walls. Interviews, magazine spreads, and television segments have brought the energy of Dutch Colony to wider audiences, capturing the essence of what makes our cafés special.

Even political figures have found a neutral ground in our cafés, where they meet with constituents over coffee. These sessions, often informal, nurture a sense of community and accessibility, allowing for open dialogue in a relaxed setting.

Through all these experiences, Dutch Colony Coffee Co. transcends the typical café model, becoming a place where coffee serves as the backdrop to life's moments, big and small.

Sustainability, Growth, and the Future of Coffee

While our cafés became gathering spaces for meaningful conversations, another important conversation naturally emerged, the one about sustainability and our role in preserving the planet. Early on, as we began sourcing our coffees from across the globe, we recognized our responsibility to ensure that each step we took left the smallest possible footprint behind.

Ethical sourcing has always been a fundamental part of Dutch Colony's story. For us, purchasing coffee beans was always personal, built on trust and genuine relationships formed with the farmers themselves. On trips to remote farms, when we can afford both time and resources to be away, be it in Indonesia or Brazil, we walked alongside farmers, observing the care they put into cultivating their land. We saw them handpick ripe cherries under the sun's heat, carefully sorting them one by one. Their faces bore smiles of pride mixed with lines of hard work, a reflection of generations of commitment to this precious craft.

Spending time at these farms changed our perspective profoundly. Sitting in modest wooden homes, sipping coffee freshly brewed by the same hands that grew it, we listened to their stories. They shared the daily challenges they faced: volatile market prices, unpredictable weather, rising production costs. Yet, their determination to maintain sustainable farming practices and care for their environment never wavered. They spoke proudly about methods like composting coffee pulp, reducing water waste, and practicing agroforestry to protect soil health and biodiversity. Every conversation deepened our appreciation and strengthened our resolve to support these practices.

Our relationship with these farmers became one of genuine friendship and mutual respect. Our fair pricing and ethical agreements represented a promise, a commitment to dignity, fairness, and collective growth. Each harvest brought us deeper into these communities, and every year, we witnessed tangible impacts. Farmers we worked closely with started investing in better infrastructure, education for their children, and even their own coffee experiments. These changes created a ripple effect across entire villages. Sustainable and ethical farming practices led to better quality, more stable incomes, and a growing sense of pride within the community. It's been an honor to contribute, even in a small way, to this journey.

Sustainability, for us, goes far beyond ethical sourcing. It is a commitment built into our daily operations, guiding the decisions we make, from how we manage waste to how we design our packaging. The choices we make behind the scenes have a lasting impact, and we have always believed that small changes, when multiplied, create meaningful progress.

One of the most pressing challenges in the café industry is waste. Every day, countless coffee grounds, milk cartons, and packaging materials are discarded, contributing to a cycle that we cannot ignore. From the beginning, we have been intentional about reducing our footprint. In our roastery, we have implemented energy-efficient roasting methods, optimizing heat usage to lower emissions. Our packaging has evolved too, as we transitioned to biodegradable bags and compostable takeaway cups, ensuring that the convenience of specialty coffee does not come at the cost of the environment.

We have also focused on finding innovative ways to repurpose what others might see as disposable. Instead of discarding used coffee grounds, we donate them to local urban farmers who use them as compost, enriching the soil with nutrients. We have collaborated with eco-conscious brands to create upcycled coffee-based skincare products, proving that sustainability and creativity can go hand in hand. And when we have surplus beans, we make sure they are donated to charities that can put them to good use, ensuring that nothing goes to waste.

But our vision goes beyond our own walls. We see Dutch Colony as part of a larger movement, one that is shaping the future of coffee culture in Singapore and overseas. Over the years, we have watched the coffee scene evolve from a niche specialty scene into something much bigger, something that excites and engages a broader audience.

Yet, there is still much to be done. The future of coffee depends on a shift in mindset that places sustainability, innovation, and community at the heart of the industry. That is the future we want to be part of, a future where businesses don't just serve great coffee but do so with responsibility, awareness, and a commitment to making a difference. Every decision, big or small, is made with one question in mind: how can we do this better for the people and the planet?

One of the moments that strengthened this philosophy was when we launched our compostable capsule range. Single-serve coffee has always presented an environmental challenge, offering convenience at the expense of sustainability. We saw a chance to change that by creating a solution that let people enjoy high-quality coffee without feeling guilty about unnecessary waste. Developing an eco-friendly alternative wasn't easy. It took research, testing, and investment in the right materials to ensure our capsules broke down naturally and still maintained the quality of our coffee.

When we brought them to market, the response was incredibly positive. Customers loved the idea of making their daily coffee habit more sustainable, which confirmed our belief that change is possible when the right choices are available. It was a small step in a much bigger movement, but it reminded us why we do what we do. And with every cup, we are working towards a future where great coffee and a great planet go hand in hand.

Besides this focus on sustainability, Dutch Colony Coffee Co. recognized that a successful business has the opportunity and the duty to make a meaningful difference in the community around it. Coffee, at its best, can empower, uplift, and create positive change. For us, that belief took the form of investing in the next generation, creating opportunities for young people to grow, thrive, and discover their potential.

An initiative close to our hearts is our partnership with TOUCH Community Services. Every few months, we gather a group of enthusiastic student-baristas from the Institute of Technical Education (ITE) colleges to introduce them to the art and science of coffee. These sessions are lively and full of curiosity. As students step into our training space for the first time, there's often a mix of nerves, excitement, and uncertainty. Many have never used a professional espresso machine before or poured steamed milk to create latte art. Some don't even drink coffee regularly.

But as we guide them through the basics, demonstrating techniques and explaining the steps with patience, something remarkable starts to happen. Nervousness gives way to fascination, hesitation turns into confidence, and soon these students are pulling espresso shots, steaming milk, and serving their creations with pride. It's inspiring to watch them stand taller as they realize they're capable of creating something beautiful and valuable.

Throughout the workshops, we aim to instill discipline, teamwork, and a sense of responsibility. Students learn the importance of consistency and quality, the art of communication with customers, and the discipline of managing a busy café environment.

Once the initial training is complete, we carefully choose a select few who show potential and a keen interest to continue their learning through internships at our cafés. These internships provide invaluable real-world experience. Interns learn how to handle the pressures of a busy service, the complexities of interacting with diverse customers, and the day-to-day challenges of operating a café. Our baristas mentor and support them closely, guiding them step by step through every process.

Over the years, we've seen incredible transformations. Shy and reserved young individuals grow into confident people with a clear vision for their future. Interns who once found it hard to make eye contact now greet regular customers with warmth and ease. Some even discover a passion for coffee and go on to secure full-time roles with Dutch Colony.

As we witnessed the impact of mentorship and hands-on experience in shaping confident professionals, we saw an opportunity to extend this to individuals who often face challenges in securing stable employment.

One of the most rewarding initiatives we embarked on was developing a structured training program for individuals with Autism Spectrum Disorder (ASD). Teaching neurodiverse individuals required a different approach—one that emphasized clarity, consistency, and patience. We adapted our training methods to provide structured, step-by-step guidance, ensuring that each skill, from operating an espresso machine to engaging with customers, was taught in a way that built confidence at a steady pace. Many of our trainees showed a natural aptitude for coffee-making, excelling in precision-driven tasks that required focus and attention to detail. Seeing them develop a sense of independence and pride in their work reinforced our belief that inclusivity in the workplace enriches not just those we train, but the entire team that learns alongside them.

Alongside this, we partnered with organizations like YMCA to support youth at risk, offering mentorship and practical training to help them find stability and purpose. Many of these young individuals have faced setbacks, with some struggling in school and others lacking a clear direction for their future. For them, coffee became a gateway to discipline, teamwork, and self-confidence. Through guided learning, hands-on practice, and the encouragement of a supportive team, we saw many grow into capable professionals, ready to take on new opportunities. These experiences remind us that investing in people is just as important as investing in coffee, and that every cup we serve carries with it the dedication, growth, and stories of those who make it possible.

Our commitment to community work also fuels us to pursue initiatives that create meaningful impact where it matters most. Being a part of the community means showing up when people need help, whether it's lending a hand to those struggling with food insecurity, taking care of our environment, or supporting causes that bring relief to those affected by crises. One of the most humbling experiences for our team has been volunteering with Meals on Wheels, delivering food to homebound individuals across Singapore. Many of the elderly and low-income families we meet rely on these meals for daily sustenance, but what makes the experience even more meaningful is the simple act of human connection. A warm conversation, a moment of recognition, and a smile exchanged at the doorstep can make as much of a difference as the meal itself. For us, it highlights that being in the service industry means truly serving people in every sense of the word.

Caring for the environment is another responsibility we take seriously. Through beach cleanup drives, we have worked with volunteers to remove waste and debris from Singapore's coastlines, ensuring that these shared spaces remain clean and beautiful for future generations.

Sustainability is an ongoing effort built into every part of our operations. From reducing single-use plastics in our cafés to repurposing used coffee jute bags for eco-friendly initiatives, we are always looking for ways to minimize waste and contribute to a healthier planet. Some of these jute bags even find a second life at the Singapore Zoo, where they are creatively repurposed for animal enrichment activities.

We have also stepped up in times of crisis. We have mobilized our resources for disaster relief efforts, running fundraising campaigns to support communities affected by floods, typhoons, and other natural disasters.

Through these initiatives, Dutch Colony aims to drive positive change, promote inclusivity, and serve as a strong support system for the community we serve.

A Quiet Reflection

Reflecting on our purpose and commitment as a business brings back memories of the tougher crossroads I faced along the way. A specific moment stands out clearly, from a time when the shine of being a new co-owner had started to wear off, replaced by the gritty reality of keeping a young business alive. It was during my second year as part of Dutch Colony when the excitement of starting something new had begun to settle into the challenging routine of daily operations and financial pressures.

I was in our tiny, cramped office at the far end of the roastery, sorting through quotations late into the evening. My phone buzzed, with a familiar name flashing on the screen. It was one of our investors, a businessman who had always shown genuine interest in the brand. He asked if we could meet, and sensing the importance in his voice, I quickly agreed.

We met in his office downtown, in a dim-lit room behind his library shelves, away from the usual busy environment. Sitting across from him, I felt an uneasy mix of curiosity and apprehension. He wasted little time, getting straight to the point with a confident smile. Leaning forward slightly, he told me that he saw huge potential for Dutch Colony, something even bigger than what we'd imagined. Then he offered a proposal: he would acquire a majority stake in our company, asking me to surrender my equity to him. He assured me that I would continue managing operations, but under his leadership, the company could scale faster, grow bigger, and become more profitable.

Sitting there, I listened quietly, my thoughts swirling. The proposal promised financial stability and rapid growth, things that at that moment felt tempting. After all, running a café and roastery meant endless uncertainties. Every day brought new pressures, unpredictable expenses, and sleepless nights spent worrying about payroll and cash flow. This offer could ease some of those burdens immediately, giving us financial security. Yet, something within me resisted. Would the company still reflect our dreams, our vision, and our commitment to the community if control shifted to someone who didn't fully share our deeper purpose?

I thanked him for his trust and promised to think about it. That night, as I walked through the roastery alone, the familiar aromas of roasted coffee lingered in the air, comforting yet sharp with clarity. I paused at our cupping table, ran my fingers over the worn wood, remembering every cupping session and every excited customer reaction to a new coffee offering.

By morning, the clarity I needed had arrived. Financial security was tempting, but not at the cost of losing what made us special—our authenticity, our independence, and our freedom to stay true to what we believed in. I knew we were not ready to compromise the soul of our business for quick growth or short-term gain.

When I finally made the call the next day to politely decline his offer, he sounded disappointed but understanding. "If you change your mind, I'm here," he said. But I knew that wouldn't happen.

Months after turning down the first offer, another one landed in our laps, this time from the chairman of one of Singapore's largest supermarket chains. It was an even bigger deal than before. He wanted to buy out all our shares, mine, Meidia's, and

Atan's, while keeping us on the board to expand Dutch Colony under his corporate umbrella. It was the kind of opportunity that could change lives overnight, the kind most entrepreneurs dream about.

We sat together, discussing it at length. On paper, it made sense. The resources, the reach, the potential to scale faster than we had ever imagined, it was all there. But as we looked at each other, we already knew the answer. Dutch Colony was never meant to be a business flipped for profit. It was our baby, one we wanted to nurture, to guide as it learned to crawl, walk, and eventually run. Selling it to someone who saw it only as a business transaction would strip it of the heart and vision that had made it what it was.

Years later, when the time finally came to close our first ever shop at Pasarbella, the 400-square-foot space where it had all begun, I found myself stepping behind the counter one last time. I pulled shots, made drinks, and chatted with customers, just as I had done in those early days. This time, I wasn't alone. My senior managers stood beside me, working through the final shift, sharing quiet moments of reflection between orders.

The space was filled with familiar faces, longtime regulars who had been with us from the start. Some shook my hand, others simply smiled, a few shared their memories of morning coffees, weekend meetups, and the friendships that had formed within these walls. One customer, someone who had been coming to Dutch Colony since the very beginning, looked at me and said, "This place is a part of people's lives now. Whatever happens next, know that you built something that truly matters."

I let those words sink in. I looked around, taking in every detail: the worn countertops, the shelves lined with coffee bags, the handwritten notes from customers pinned to the board. This was a piece of our story.

As I stepped out of Pasarbella for the last time, I felt nothing but certainty. We had made the right choices, even when they were difficult. We had stayed true to our vision, even when easier paths were laid out before us. Today, as I walk into any of our cafés, I see what we have created. A space filled with warmth, a brand people trust, a business that has stood the test of time because of passion, perseverance, and a belief in doing things the right way. Dutch Colony Coffee Co. is a story of resilience, community, and heart. And as long as we hold on to that, I know we'll always be exactly where we're meant to be.

Bonus Section

Conversations with My Partner: Atan Chua

No story of Dutch Colony Coffee Co. can be told without the spirit of collaboration that built it. This journey was never mine alone; it was shaped by the conversations, the challenges, and the shared moments with my partners. Over the years, we have exchanged thoughts over many cups of coffee, debated decisions that would steer the business, and stood by each other through every high and low. Some of these conversations were filled with excitement, others with tough truths, and some even with silence, where words weren't needed to understand what was at stake.

As I penned this chapter, I found myself revisiting many of these moments, consulting both my partners along the way. Their voices are as much a part of this story as mine, and in this bonus section, I wanted to share a glimpse into one of my conversations with my co-partner Atan Chua, a candid reflection on our journey, our challenges, and what this company truly means to us.

Me: *"I remember how it all began—the first time we connected. Atan, you were in the U.S. and introduced me to Stumptown Cold Brew in a bottle, and that's where the spark of collaboration and the friendship first ignited. At that time, we had no idea where this would all go, but the idea of bringing that experience to Singapore was a shared vision that set us on the path to building something special.*

Before I officially joined DCC, we spent countless hours chatting over Facebook Messenger. You mentioned that Meidia was already noticing me and connecting, but somehow, it felt like you were the one talking to me the most. Maybe it was those late-night discussions, where we spoke about everything under the sun—what you both wanted to do with the brand, the challenges you anticipated, and the opportunities you both saw. It felt like we were already partners, long before the formalities of joining DCC."

On February 4, 2014, I remember you saying something that stuck with me: "So, again, we don't want to take away anything...and we are hoping that if you decide, it's also because you believe in DCC...in us." Those words resonated deeply. It wasn't just about business; it was about belief—belief in each other, belief in the vision we were creating. It was the moment I knew that Dutch Colony wasn't just another project—it was a family, one that would work together to build something meaningful.

Me: *Soon after, I came on board, while you were still helping out on a part-time basis and on weekends, while juggling your day job. We then spoke often about what Meidia and I needed from you, and what value you could bring, if you come in fully on board. Even when we discussed you potentially joining full-time, we talked about how we could complement each other. I said, "If you come in, I think all of us can work based on our strengths." That conversation was a turning point for us all, and you fully came in. I realized that each of us brought something unique to the table. It wasn't just about our skills—it was about our shared passions, our vision for the brand, and our commitment to making Dutch Colony a place where people felt something more than just a cup of coffee.*

Atan:I'll never forget the day we talked about Acaia. It was May 27, 2014, and we were discussing the idea of getting the distributorship of weighing scales. It seemed like a small conversation at the time, but little did we know, that was the beginning of our journey with Acaia. That partnership opened up new doors for us, and now, it feels like a natural part of who we are. It's a symbol of how our conversations often lead to real action—ideas that turn into milestones, just like our long discussions on how to take DCC to the next level.

But what really set the tone for our partnership was the way we supported each other, not just in business, but in life. There were moments when we weren't just partners in coffee—we were partners in life. When your dad had to go through his medical check-up, when he was hospitalized, and later, when he passed away, you mentioned that I was always there. You mentioned too that we were more than business partners—we were family, offering support, understanding, and accommodation during the toughest moments of everyone's life. And when one of us faced challenges with the family's financial commitments, we discussed and agreed to use the GWO fund to help, showing each other trust and commitment to the team.

One of the most rewarding moments came when we finally saw our dream come to fruition: the Loring roaster. After almost six years of planning, we received the unit just before the pandemic hit. Watching my excitement was like seeing a kid get their favorite candy. You mentioned my passion and dedication were infectious, and that I made sure everything was in place, putting my heart into it. That moment was a testament to how far we'd come, from that first cold brew to standing in front of our own Loring, a symbol of the hard work, the dedication, and the belief we had in our vision.

And then, of course, there were the dark times—the challenges we faced as a company. There's no need to dwell on the specifics, but I think we all know how we weathered those storms together. We learned, we grew, and we came out stronger on the other side. Even in those moments, we never wavered in our commitment to each other, to the company, and to the dream we were building. And that's what makes this journey so special.

Reflecting on these conversations, it's clear that what we've built together goes far beyond the business. Dutch Colony is not just about coffee—it's about people, relationships, and a shared belief in the power of community. We've taken care of each other, supported each other, and built something we can all be proud of. It's not just a partnership—it's family. And that, I think, is the secret to why Dutch Colony is what it is today.

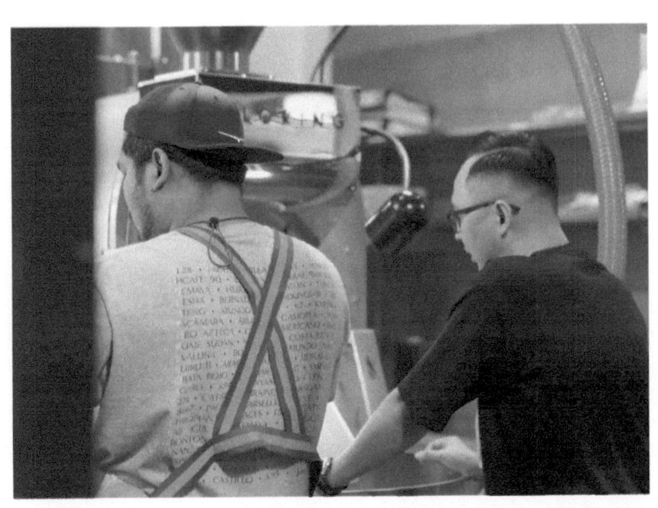

EXIT

SB052510

CONCLUSION

A Legacy Still Brewing

Sometimes, when the café empties after a busy afternoon, and the gentle sounds of chatter slowly fades, I find myself drifting back in time. In those quiet pauses, I remember the first time I truly tasted kopi. It was a sleepy Saturday morning at my grandparents' place, my hands trembling as I carefully sipped the black gold from the delicate saucer my Atuk handed me.

From that innocent moment, who could have imagined how my story and Singapore's coffee story would unfold. Back then, our city was dotted with humble kopitiams, places brimming with warmth and tradition. The same kopitiams on every street corner, the same kopi poured with the same technique, the same comfort of watching my Atuk or Ayah exchange easy conversations with the uncle behind the counter. I still remember sitting at a worn-out wooden table, surrounded by the scent of condensed milk and roasted beans, watching as the kopitiam uncles worked their magic.

It was in one of those kopitiams, my legs barely reaching the floor, that I declared with all the confidence of a child, "Maybe, one day I'll become a kopi master too." Atuk's friends around us laughed, their voices bouncing off the tiled walls, their hands clapping my back in amusement. I can still hear those echoes, and now, all these years later, I smile to myself. Some dreams take their own shape, unfolding in ways we never quite expect, just like Singapore's caffeine-fueled transformation. The drink that once carried the weight of nostalgia began to take on new dimensions: a craft, an art, an entire movement built on passion and innovation.

Today, coffee is a conversation between cultures, an experience shaped by both tradition and modernity, and an ever-evolving art form. Walk through the city and you'll see it everywhere, the old and the new coexisting in a way that feels seamless. The familiar sight of uncles sipping their kopi O at a corner kopitiam remains unchanged, while a few streets away a barista meticulously prepares a single-origin pour-over, weighing every gram and timing every extraction with precision.

This, to me, is the heart of Singapore's coffee story: how we have preserved the soul of our past while making space for new ideas, flavors, and experiences. It isn't about choosing one over the other. It is about celebrating the full spectrum of what coffee can be, allowing it to evolve without forgetting where it began.

Looking ahead, coffee continues to evolve at a remarkable pace. It has become a reflection of individual taste, an extension of personal identity. The way people engage with coffee has changed. People are no longer content with just drinking it; they want to understand it, personalize it, and even take part in the process. The future of coffee will be shaped by this shift toward customization, where baristas and technology work together to create tailored experiences for every coffee lover.

Precision brewing, AI-assisted roasting, and advanced extraction techniques are already here, reshaping how we cultivate, process, and brew coffee. The innovations we once marveled at are now shaping everyday experiences. As a coffee professional, this excites me because it reassures me that coffee will never be stagnant, that it will keep pushing boundaries, inviting us to rethink what we know, and challenging us to be better.

Despite all the advancements and innovations, coffee remains, at its core, something far more profound than a drink. It has always been a bridge that connects people, stories, and cultures. In a world that often feels fragmented, coffee offers something rare: a reason to slow down, to share a moment, and to engage with one another in a way that feels unhurried and real.

It creates spaces where conversations unfold naturally, where strangers become friends, and where connections deepen over something as simple as a shared cup. Whether it's in a spirited café, a quiet kopitiam, or the comfort of home, coffee brings people together in ways that transcend backgrounds and differences. Some of the most meaningful conversations I've ever had, whether about business, life, or dreams yet to be realized, have been over coffee. It has a way of stripping away the noise and distractions, leaving room for something more honest and more human.

As coffee culture continues to evolve, it becomes increasingly clear that its future is about more than taste and technique. It is about responsibility. People today are asking bigger questions. Where does their coffee come from? Who grows it? What impact does it leave behind? These questions are part of a collective awakening. Coffee lovers are no longer satisfied with simply enjoying a good cup; they want to know that it has been sourced ethically, that the farmers who cultivate it are treated fairly, and that the process does not come at the cost of the planet's well-being.

The choices we make now will shape the future of coffee for generations to come. From farm to cup, every decision holds weight. Sustainability is an obligation. From ethical sourcing and waste reduction to innovating for a lower carbon footprint, every coffee professional has a responsibility to help this craft we love thrive. And so, I find myself returning to one crucial question: ***What kind of legacy do we want coffee to leave behind?***

As I ponder this, I am compelled to think about how crucial it is in a coffee city. But what truly defines a coffee city? It isn't the cafes dotting the streets or the bags of beans neatly lined up on shelves that first come to mind. Instead, I see faces: the people who bring coffee to life, the baristas who stand patiently behind the counters, the farmers who rise before dawn, tending their crops with dedication, the roasters carefully adjusting heat and airflow, chasing that ideal flavor, and the countless customers who gather around tables, turning ordinary days into special memories.

Singapore might be small in size, but in spirit, our coffee scene pulses with life. It has quietly become a place of influence, where conversations about quality, sustainability, and community echo far beyond our shores. We might not have sprawling coffee plantations like Ethiopia, Brazil, or Colombia, but we have something equally significant, an understanding that coffee, at its heart, is about people. Coffee in Singapore embodies who we are. Each sip we take is a tribute, celebrating the past, embracing the present, and paving the path forward.

So, the next time you wrap your hands around your favorite coffee mug, feel its warmth, and pause to inhale its rich aroma, remember this: you are part of a story far greater than a single moment. You are joining a conversation that spans continents and generations, a story shared through quiet nods exchanged in crowded coffee shops, through the soft laughter between old friends catching up, through thoughtful discussions and inspiring ideas sparked over countless cups.

As Aristotle once said, "The essence of life is to serve others and do good." And perhaps, in sharing coffee, in creating spaces for connection, in honoring the work that goes into every bean, we are doing just that. We nourish connections. We strengthen communities. We plant seeds of hope and goodness that continue growing long after the last drop is gone. In the end, coffee is about the lives it touches, the communities it supports, and the legacy it leaves behind.

And that legacy is still brewing.

A Note From the Author

As we wrap up this journey we've taken together through the intriguing and inspiring world of coffee, I wanted to pause for a moment and speak to you directly, heart to heart. Writing this book, my very first, has been about offering a glimpse into the deeper community that has formed around coffee, the lives it has touched, and the ways it has shaped us all.

Reflecting on this journey has been unexpectedly emotional. I've spent many evenings sitting quietly at my desk, lost in memories that resurfaced vividly as I revisited moments of joy, struggle, and growth.

When I first decided to write this book, I thought my previous experience writing articles and blogs on coffee would make it easier. After all, I'd spent years capturing my thoughts in short pieces and connecting with readers who encouraged me to take this bigger leap. But I soon discovered that writing a book required something different, something deeper. Determined to do this the right way, I dove into learning. I signed up for online courses, devoured books on writing, and studied different styles to refine my own voice. But no matter how much I prepared, I found myself constantly questioning if it was enough. So I pushed further, bringing in a book publisher and a writing coach to guide me through the final stages.

There were late nights spent piecing together memories, retracing steps, and revisiting conversations that shaped the moments that mattered most. Some nights, the words flowed effortlessly, while on others, I found myself staring at a blinking cursor, filled with doubts. Would anyone care to read the reflections of a first-time author? Would my experiences resonate beyond the world of coffee? Those doubts crept in often, but every time they did, I reminded myself why I had started writing this in the first place: to honor the journey, to document the lessons, and to share a story that might inspire someone else to chase their own path in coffee, business, or life.

At the same time, life didn't slow down just because I had taken on the challenge of writing a book. There were responsibilities waiting for me outside of these pages, the daily demands of running a business, leading a team, and, above all, being present for my family. I was still a husband, a father, and a son, juggling the roles that mattered most. Writing often took a backseat to bedtime stories, family dinners, and the countless decisions that came with leading Dutch Colony. There were days when I wished I could dedicate uninterrupted time to finish the book faster, but looking back, I realize that it unfolded exactly as it was meant to.

This book could have been completed years earlier if I had isolated myself from the distractions, but then it would have been missing something important: the wisdom gained through those very distractions. The experiences, the setbacks, and the moments that forced me to pause all shaped the perspective I bring to these pages.

This journey was also driven by something deeper than personal ambition, it was the will of Allah swt, guiding every step I took. My faith has been a steady anchor, offering me strength when motivation ran low and clarity when the road ahead felt uncertain. The process of putting words on paper turned into a spiritual practice, reinforcing my connection to God and my commitment to serving Him with sincerity. Every word, every late night, every moment of doubt was gently eased by the presence and grace of Allah swt, guiding me forward even when the journey felt overwhelming. In that way, this book is a humble reflection of His will, and I am grateful for the chance to share it.

This book is dedicated to every barista patiently pulling espresso shots, perfecting latte art, and caring deeply about their craft. It is dedicated to home brewers who wake up before sunrise, quietly working on their pour-over in the calm of dawn. It is written for farmers who lovingly grow, harvest, and prepare the beans that form the foundation of every cup we cherish. It is for the customers who take time to pause, reflect, and appreciate the fleeting moments life offers in the quiet corners of their favorite café. Most importantly, it is dedicated to the community: the family brought together by a shared love for coffee, united in the belief that it is more than a drink, it is a beautiful way of life.

I genuinely hope this book finds its way into your hands for a meaningful reason, whether it's curiosity, a desire to learn, or simply to feel more connected to coffee's intricate and inspiring world. If it gives you a moment of contemplation, sparks a new thought, or helps deepen your appreciation for coffee, then it has truly served its purpose.

While this marks the completion of my first book, I sense it is the start of something even bigger. It feels like the first step in a continuing journey, filled with more stories, more discoveries, and more cups of coffee shared with warmth.

Here's to coffee, to community, to stories shared, and to many more still waiting to unfold.

Thank you for walking this journey with me.

Acknowledgements

B-ismi-llāhi r-raḥmāni r-raḥīmi بِسْمِ اللهِ الرَّحْمٰنِ الرَّحِيْمِ

In the name of God, the Most Gracious, the Most Merciful.

As I write these final words, I pause, not out of hesitation, but in deep gratitude. This book exists because of the love, sacrifices, and encouragement of so many people who have been part of this journey, whether knowingly or unknowingly. Some have stood by me through every step, offering strength and guidance, while others have influenced my path in ways they may never fully realize. Their presence, their wisdom, and their belief in me have shaped these pages in more ways than I can count.

To my beloved wife and children, Karmila, Qistina Quraisya, Adam Qushayri, Qalesya Sakinah, and Sadeeq Qayyim, you are the foundation upon which my dreams stand. Your patience, your understanding, and your unwavering love have given me the strength to see this journey through. Every late night spent writing, every weekend devoted to refining my thoughts, every moment of uncertainty, you were there, grounding me, reminding me why this mattered. There were times when the weight of this project felt overwhelming, but knowing I had you to come home to make all the difference.

A special mention to my wife, Karmila— a strong, inspiring woman who made the profound sacrifice of putting aside her personal goals and professional ambitions to be a full-time mom.

Your selflessness allowed me the space to focus and flourish, and for that, I am endlessly grateful.

To my parents, Sukiman Satari and Hamidah Attan (Ayu), Ayah and Mak, your love has always been my anchor, even when I didn't fully understand it. I know my journey took a different path from what you had envisioned, but your guidance and prayers never wavered. Your concern, your quiet sacrifices, and your constant presence have shaped me in ways I can never fully express. When you gave me your blessing to pursue this passion, it felt like a door had opened, one that allowed me to step forward with confidence. I carry your prayers with me in everything I do, and I hope this book reflects the values, strength, and perseverance you have instilled in me.

To my parents-in-law, Kamis Bin Saidi (Papa) and Salimah Bte Jaafar (Mama), thank you for raising a daughter whose patience, integrity, and faith have deeply shaped my growth as a husband and father. In our early years, when we struggled as new parents, they selflessly stepped in to care for our daughter so we could focus on our work. Despite my father-in-law's challenges now, as he faces a brain stroke and memory loss, he continues to ask, 'Everything is under control, Boss?'—a phrase that holds even more meaning today. My mother-in-law, though frail, remains a constant source of quiet strength, always supporting my wife and encouraging her to stand by me. Their love and support have been invaluable, and I am forever grateful.

To my past bosses, each of you played a role in my growth, whether through mentorship, challenges, or hard-earned lessons. Leadership, patience, and perseverance were not just concepts I learned; they were qualities I developed under your guidance. Every opportunity, every piece of advice, and even the toughest moments along the way helped shape who I am today. Yolande Woo, Syd Ahmad, Kimberly Yer, Burger Ang, Alex Chong, Toby Smith, and Andrew Low, you have all left an imprint on my journey, and for that, I will always be grateful.

To my business partners, Atan Chua and Meidia Tamboto, you have been more than colleagues. You have been co-architects of a vision that continues to take shape, evolve, and inspire. Thank you for believing in me, for standing together in both the victories and the hardships, and for staying true to the values that built this journey. What we have is a shared dream, a commitment to something greater than ourselves, and an ongoing story that we continue to write together.

To my partners in crime, my steadfast Dutch Colony brothers, Zuhaimi Zu and Nazrul, there are no words that could fully capture my gratitude. You have stood by me in every season, in every moment that tested our resilience. Through long nights, ambitious goals, and the grind that never stops, you have been more than colleagues. You have been family. We have built a culture, a purpose, and a decade of dedication that has shaped not just our careers, but our lives.

To the late Roger Smith and Grant Rattray, two coffee legends whose absence is deeply felt, but whose impact remains alive in the hearts of those they mentored. Roger, as Chairman of Toby's Estate and father of its founder, left an imprint on the coffee world that will continue to be felt for generations. His presence was one of wisdom, strength, and an unwavering belief in the craft. Grant, with his remarkable knowledge of coffee farming and an approach to cupping that turned tasting into an art, had a way of making every conversation about coffee feel like a journey. Learning from them was one of the great privileges of my career. They were larger than life in their expertise, generosity of spirit, and in the way they made coffee personal and meaningful.

This book is dedicated to them both. Their legacy lives on, in every lesson they imparted, in every person they inspired, and in every cup of coffee that carries the depth of their passion. I can only hope to honor their memory by continuing to serve, to learn, and to give back, just as they did.

To the countless individuals who have shaped my journey, the farmers whose dedication and care cultivate the very beans I cherish, the roasters who transform potential into exceptional coffees, the baristas who craft each cup with skill and warmth, and the customers whose appreciation inspires us all, I offer my heartfelt gratitude. This book belongs to each of you, a reflection of a shared pursuit of excellence and passion within our global coffee family.

To Dutch Colony Coffee Co. and our larger team, you have created a place of creativity, growth, and community. The insights gained, the friendships formed, and the values nurtured in our shared space have influenced my understanding of coffee's true essence. Coffee has become our common language, bridging differences, sparking meaningful conversations, and fueling a powerful movement. I hope this book captures the essence of everything we've built and achieved together.

To everyone who has stood by me, encouraged me, and believed in my vision, this accomplishment is yours as much as it is mine. May it remind us all that dreams flourish when shared, and true success comes from walking hand in hand with others who lift us up.

Most importantly, my deepest gratitude goes to Allah SWT. Every sentence in this book, every insight offered, and every moment of inspiration came from His boundless mercy and guidance. He instilled in my heart the desire to start this journey, granted me the endurance to see it through, and provided the wisdom to reach its completion. My prayer is that this book fulfills its purpose, touches those who read it, and serves as a means for lasting goodness. Alhamdulillah, for without His divine guidance, none of this would have come to fruition.

Photo Credits

The photographs in this book are a testament to the vibrant coffee culture and the incredible people behind it. I would like to extend my heartfelt gratitude to the talented photographers and organizations who have contributed their work to bring this book to life.

Photographers:

- Andrew Hoi
- Atan Chua
- Anuar Khairullah

Organizations:

- Singapore Coffee Association
- Thailand Coffee Association
- Malaysia Coffee Association
- Indonesia Coffee Association

Their keen eye and dedication to capturing the essence of coffee have enriched these pages, adding depth to the stories told. Thank you for being part of this journey.

About the Author: Suhaimi Sukiman

Suhaimi Sukiman's journey in coffee has embraced both the old and the new of Singapore's coffee culture. From his early days frequenting kopitiams with his Atuk and Ayah, watching kopi being pulled, to stepping behind the counter as a young barista at Starbucks, his love for coffee grew alongside the city's evolving coffee scene.

After serving his national duty, he returned to Starbucks in 2005, this time as a manager. It was here that he developed a strong foundation in leadership and training, evolving to become a Classroom Facilitator and eventually a Coffee Ambassador for Starbucks Singapore in his final year with the Siren. His drive to learn soon led him to Cuppachoice International in 2007, a specialty coffee roastery where he immersed himself in roasting and coffee sales. Through perseverance, he climbed the ranks from Executive to Director of Operations and Training by 2010.

He also became a competitive barista, placing third in the Singapore National Barista Championship in 2010 and 2011, and third again in the Singapore National Latte Art Championship in 2011. His expertise expanded when he joined Toby's Estate in 2011, traveling to coffee farms and judging competitions. In 2013, he achieved a career milestone: becoming one of 55 globally certified World Barista Championship judges.

In 2014, Suhaimi became a co-partner at Dutch Colony Coffee Co., overseeing sourcing, roasting, and education. Under his leadership, Dutch Colony expanded regionally, supplying coffee to multiple countries. He also became an AST Trainer with the Specialty Coffee Association and continued judging world-sanctioned competitions.

From barista to roaster, competitor to entrepreneur, Suhaimi's journey reflects a lifelong commitment to coffee. Today, he remains dedicated to elevating the craft, growing Dutch Colony, and inspiring the next generation of coffee professionals.

www.ingramcontent.com/pod-product-compliance
Ingram Content Group UK Ltd.
Pitfield, Milton Keynes, MK11 3LW, UK
UKHW041631190726
13854UKWH00006B/2427